Advice for Recovering Your Inner Strength &
Spirit from the World's Most Famous Survivors

HEALING

J. Pincott, editor

Random House Reference
New York · Toronto · London · Sydney · Auckland

Please address inquiries about electronic licensing of any products for use on a network, in software, or on CD-ROM to the Subsidiary Rights Department, Random House Information Group, fax 212-572-6003.

This book is available at special discounts for bulk purchases for sales promotions or premiums. Special editions, including personalized covers, excerpts of existing books, and corporate imprints, can be created in large quantities for special needs. For more information, write to Random House, Inc., Special Markets/Premium Sales, 1745 Broadway, MD 6-2, New York, NY 10019 or e-mail specialmarkets@randomhouse.com.

Visit the Random House Reference Web site:
www.randomwords.com

Library of Congress Cataloging-in-Publication Data

Healing : advice for recovering your strength and spirit from the world's most famous survivors / J. Pincott, editor.
    p. cm.
  Includes bibliographical references.
  ISBN 978-0-375-42611-7 (hardcover : alk. paper)
1. Life change events—Psychological aspects. 2. Healing.
3. Life—Quotations, maxims, etc. 4. Life skills—
Quotations, maxims, etc.   I. Pincott, J. (Jena)
  BF637.L53H42 2007
  155.9'3—dc22   2007019965

Printed in the United States of America

10 9 8 7 6 5 4 3 2 1

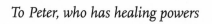

To Peter, who has healing powers

It is easy to go down into Hell;
night and day, the gates
of dark Death stand wide; but
to climb back again,
to retrace one's steps to
the upper air—there's the rub,
the task.

–Virgil, poet

CONTENTS

INTRODUCTION

Of families, Leo Tolstoy famously observed: "happy ones are all alike, unhappy ones are unhappy in their own ways." The same can be said of individuals: happy ones feel connected to others, unhappy ones feel alone in their suffering. Depression, heartbreak, betrayal, abuse, illness, accidents, miscarriage, rejection, career setbacks, divorce, drug and alcohol addiction, the death of loved ones, and so on are so personally devastating that those experiencing them often believe others couldn't possibly relate.

But it's not true. With more than six billion people on the planet, there's a pretty good chance that others share similar hardships. And among us are survivors—

those who have endured physical and emotional pain and come out wiser. Those who managed to heal.

Healing is a collection of insights and advice from such survivors. I have trawled through interviews, articles, broadcasts, autobiographies, and speeches to find advice and insights on the healing process. Many of the people quoted in this book are well-known business leaders, actors and actresses, singers, writers, artists, and philosophers.

Included here are Steve Jobs on what he learned from his cancer diagnosis, Elton John on rebounding from drug and alcohol addiction, Hilary Swank on surviving divorce, and Bruce Willis on accepting the death of his brother. Here, too, are Gladys Knight on coping with her son's death, Patch Adams on generating hope, Kylie Minogue on beating breast cancer, Sharon Stone on surviving a near-death experience, and Eva Kor on forgiving the Nazi doctors who violated her during the Holocaust. These survivors and others have used their fame as a platform to talk about how they survived, and in some cases thrived, in the aftermath of personal tragedy.

We heal in a variety of ways: by accepting, believing, changing, connecting, coping, creating, forgiving, laughing, living, persisting, and transcending. These are the themes of this book. Many of the excerpts focus on finding a reason and purpose for your problem ("When you understand there is a purpose, then you can handle a lot of stuff."—Rick Warren). Others offer specific remedies for mind and spirit ("No matter what you're going through, pick up a phone and call somebody at home [who's] sick, or go down to the shelter and help somebody learn to read."—Laura Schlesinger). Many address life changes ("Remembering that you are going to die is the best way I know to avoid the trap of thinking you have something to lose. There is no reason not to follow your heart."—Steve Jobs.) Others address the healing virtues of spirituality ("You're born.

You suffer. You die. Fortunately, there's a loophole."—Billy Graham).

My hope is that *Healing* will be a salve for sufferers. Use it to help distance yourself from your problem, or at least understand it better. More importantly, may the ideas and advice of these survivors remind you that suffering can be overcome. Even Tolstoy, whose characters are often the embodiment of human misery and tragedy, believed this. He wrote, "The most difficult thing of all—yet the most essential—is to love life, even when you suffer, because life is all."

Acceptance is commonly

known as the final stage of grief (after denial, anger, bargaining, and depression). It's also the first stage of healing. Only after you've accepted your situation can you begin to recover from it.

Look at it this way: The storm has passed. Your personal landscape has changed. But you're beginning to accept the new terrain, the new reality.

You're beginning to heal.

ACCEPTING

❦

Not everything that is faced can be changed,
but nothing can be changed until it is faced.
—**James Baldwin**, *author*

❦

You have got to want to admit that you
have got a problem, first of all. Then start to
deal with why that is.
—**Mary J. Blige**, *singer–songwriter*

❦

You're not going to live your life unscathed.
—**Kirstie Alley**, *actress*

❦

BE STRONGER THAN YOU KNOW

In the moment, life's setbacks—sickness, death of a loved one, career setbacks, fractured relationships, and so on—may seem permanently disabling. But everyone goes through them at some point, and their lives go on, perhaps altered but not broken. People are hardwired to survive. You're tougher than you think.

One of my favorite lines from [a] book that I have always loved is, "Life is difficult from the road less traveled." That's the first line of that book. And life is difficult. I think most people have the expectation that it's supposed to always be happy. But if you're an adult, you know that there are always valleys and mountains. And at some point, many of us will face life-challenging trials that knock us to the ground. And what I know is that it's how we pick ourselves back up, how you take that pain and you turn it into something powerful for yourself and for other people, that really matters. You are stronger than you know.

—*Oprah Winfrey,* talk-show host

Most people live, whether physically, intellectually or morally, in a very restricted circle of their potential being. They make use of a very small portion of their possible consciousness, and of their soul's resources in general, much like a man who, out of his whole bodily organism, should get into a habit of using and moving only his little finger. Great emergencies and crises show us how much greater our vital resources are than we had supposed.

—*William James,* psychologist and philosopher

I think everybody has tragedy in their life. Everybody has hurdles in their life. Everybody has tough things to overcome. My kids say to me, "This isn't fair." I said, "Life isn't fair." Everybody has their issues. It's how you handle your issues that distinguishes you. . . .

—*Maria Shriver,* journalist and niece of the late President John F. Kennedy

You need to accept your situation if you want to be empowered to change it. . . . Once you accept that the disease or other misfortune has become a part of your life, you can marshal your forces to eliminate or alter it. If you avoid thinking about it, deny it or feel hopeless, you cannot play a part in changing it and your life. Accepting the situation does not mean accepting someone else's prediction about what will happen to you. No one knows what your future will be. . . . Individuals are not statistics.

—**Bernie Siegel**, surgeon and writer

People go through challenging moments of losing people and of having their life threatened from illness and real grief. But they get through it. And that's the testament to the human spirit—we are fragile, but we also are divine.

—*Sheryl Crow,* singer–songwriter, *on recovering from breast cancer*

You may surprise yourself with your ability cope to with, and eventually accept, even the most challenging situations.

Last year was a very, very difficult year for me because my daughter was very sick. She was in a coma. If you had told me the day before she fell into the coma that such a thing was going to happen, I would have killed myself. If I had known the amount of pain I would have to endure, I would have killed myself because I would have thought I would never be able to survive this thing—and I wouldn't have wanted to survive; I would have wanted to die before.

But then, one day at a time, you take it. You go through one week, and the next week; the whole year goes by. And things happen that are so horrible, and they get worse and worse. You think you are going to die at every step, but you don't die. You survive.

—*Isabel Allende*, writer, *on coping after her daughter died of porphyria*

Acceptance can be an act of courage and self-love.

I'm fine, and my hips are fine. My false knee is fine. My false hips are fine.

—*Liza Minnelli*, actress

My [mastectomy] scar is beautiful. It looks like an arrow. I didn't bother rubbing things into it or having any silicone injections. . . . I thought of having a designer make a beautiful dress with cutouts here [points at scar] and doing a picture of me wearing it. I just want to show off my scar proudly and not be afraid of it. A really strong woman accepts the war she went through and is ennobled by her scars.

—*Carly Simon*, singer, *on recovering from breast cancer*

Terrible things can happen to us, rape, accident, bereavement; life is precarious and full of the unexpected, but we do not have to become victims, no matter what happens. That is a choice, and one we do not have to make. If we choose to remain ourselves, full of potential, then we can take whatever happens and redeem it by openness, courage, and willingness to move on.

—*Madeleine L'Engle,* writer, *who suffered from a serious injury in an automobile accident*

I've never tried to block out the memories of the past, even though some are painful. I don't understand people who hide from their past. Everything you live through helps to make you the person you are now.

—*Sophia Loren,* actress

You cannot prevent the birds of sorrow from flying over your head, but you can prevent them from building nests in your hair.

—Chinese proverb

LOOK FOR A PURPOSE

It may be easier to accept a setback if you can ascribe purpose to it. If you can find reason or redemption in it, it's easier to understand and accept.

To live is to suffer, to survive is to find some meaning in the suffering.
—*Roberta Flack*, singer

You can handle almost anything in life if you know there is a purpose behind it. That's the real key. When there is a purpose behind it— pain is hard to handle if you don't see any purpose in it. When you understand there is a purpose, then you can handle a lot of stuff.
—*Rick Warren*, minister and author

You will not grow if you sit in a beautiful flower garden, but you will grow if you are sick, if you are in pain, if you experience losses, and if you do not put your head in the sand, but take the pain as a gift to you with a very, very specific purpose.
—*Elizabeth Kubler-Ross*, psychiatrist and author

Whenever someone sorrows, I do not say, "forget it" or "it will pass" or "it could be worse"—all of which deny the integrity of the painful experience. But I say, to the contrary, "It is worse than you may allow yourself to think. Delve into the depth. Stay with the feeling. Think of it as a precious source of knowledge and guidance. Then and only then will you be ready to face it and be transformed in the process."

—*Peter Koestenbaum,* philosopher and consultant

∽

Without pain, there would be no suffering, without suffering we would never learn from our mistakes. To make it right, pain and suffering is the key to all windows, without it, there is no way of life.

—*Angelina Jolie,* actress

It's a difficult question, but it's worth asking yourself. Can you find any purpose in your pain?

Pain is meant to wake us up. People try to hide their pain. But they're wrong. Pain is something to carry, like a radio. You feel your strength in the experience of pain. It's all in how you carry it. That's what matters. Pain is a feeling. Your feelings are a part of you. Your own reality. If you feel ashamed of them, and hide them, you're letting society destroy your reality. You should stand up for your right to feel your pain.

—*Jim Morrison,* singer–songwriter

༄

Illness, loss of loved ones, disappointment, decline, death, limitations, and imperfections startle and shake us. But they awaken us to find meaning, dignity, and significance in our lives. They open the heart to pure compassion and newfound creative energy . . . .Real suffering is useful. It propels us to new levels of consciousness and self-knowledge.

—*Kathleen Brehony,* psychologist and personal coach

༄

[By having polio] I developed certain survival skills. By the end of it all, I had experienced something that has served me well throughout my life. I had had to deal with the precariousness of our place in the world and to understand something about healing and how to endure its processes. Without that polio experience, I really think I might not have weathered so many of the changes that would follow. . . . When I was thirteen, my older brother died in a plane crash. And then, when I was seventeen, my father died. All of these worlds that were familiar to me as a child were dealt a series of blows.

—*Mia Farrow,* actress, *on recovering from childhood polio*

One thing I will say is that I went to a really dark place and made it back, and I'm humbled by it and super-grateful to be where I am. I think what makes people unique are their experiences, the things we have to draw from, and as an actor I have so many amazing and beautiful things to draw from. Even though a lot of it was dark, a lot of it was great and wild and interesting.

—*Balthazar Getty,* actor, *on overcoming drug addiction*

CHOOSE YOUR FOCUS

If you focus on suffering, that's all you'll experience. It will take over your life. You may not have control over your situation, but you can choose how you perceive it and react to it. By accepting your situation you've decided to shift your focus to other facets of your life.

Life is a train of moods like a string of beads; and as we pass through them they prove to be many colored lenses, which paint the world their own hue, and each shows us only what lies in its own focus.

—*Ralph Waldo Emerson,* philosopher and writer

In the end, it just didn't work, but I would never look back on this relationship as failed. I look at it as 13 1/2 years of success.

—*Hilary Swank,* actress, *on healing from divorce*

You are in charge of how you react to the people and events in your life. You can either give negativity power over your life or you can choose happiness instead. Take control and choose to focus on what is important in your life. Those who cannot live fully often become destroyers of life.

—Anaïs Nin, writer

You might cry. You might even cry so much that there are no tears left, but still your grief lets you make decisions and you grow as a person. Everything depends upon how you handle it. Whether you accept your grief, your loss and your mourning or whether you try to push it away. I think you have to live it up.

—**Tori Amos,** singer, *on recovering from a miscarriage*

It's all a matter of what you train your eyes to see, and a willingness to embrace it all: the dark and the light. I try to write from this perspective. Our hearts are broken daily. And they are mended again. The heart is meant to be broken, so that a huge tree can grow out of it. Our tears water the dry places in the heart so the tree can grow wide and wild, and with all kinds of creatures living in it.

—**Rebecca Wells,** actress, writer, and survivor of severe neurological Lyme disease

In moments of discouragement, defeat, or even despair, there are always certain things to cling to. Little things usually: remembered laughter, the face of a sleeping child, a tree in the wind—in fact, any reminder of something deeply felt or dearly loved. No man is so poor as not to have many of these small candles. When they are lighted, darkness goes away—and a touch of wonder remains.

—**Arthur Gordon**, writer and polio survivor

Accept your situation, then choose where and how to focus your energy.

I remember hearing a quote from [tennis champion] Arthur Ashe when he was stricken with HIV. He said, "I'm not going to sit here and say 'Why me?' because I wasn't saying 'Why me?' when I was holding up the Wimbledon trophy. . . . So many people get so many good things, and they don't think, 'Why me? Why am I so lucky?' So you really shouldn't think, 'Why am I so unlucky?' Because I had so many things go right in my life up until last year, that I'm—you know, I'm bound for a little bit of rain amongst the sunshine."

—*James Blake,* tennis player, *on his role model Arthur Ashe's acceptance of having contracted HIV from a blood transfusion*

Life goes through changes so fast, you think your life is great, then one of your best friends dies. Then you think you found someone you truly love, only to figure out, she doesn't love you back. You cry and cry and cry, but nothing changes. You realize, that you must accept things for what they are, and what they have made you become. Everything in life changes you in some way. Even the smallest things. If you do not accept these changes, you do not accept yourself. For through these changes brings new and greater things to you, making you wiser, as time progresses. To avoid these changes is a loss.

—*Adam Gwizdala,* writer

✍

. . . Make a gratitude list. This helps me—it's like the old saying, count your blessings, it's so silly, but it is true. Whenever I get depressed, which is a lot, I go okay, but . . . I am living in a free country. I am not in pain. I just go down the list, and nature feeds me. I just go outside and I look at trees or the mountains or the ocean, just try to connect with nature. I just go things are bad, but good lord, look what I have.

—*Fannie Flagg,* writer and actress

Try to train not only your thoughts but also the words that embody those thoughts. Language shapes your perceptions.

Be careful about the language you use. When you use catastrophic terms like "nightmare," "terrible," and "horrible," you're bound to spend time dwelling on the negative. Focus on what you can do.

—*Dr. Phillip (Phil) McGraw,* psychologist and television personality, *on recovering from a broken heart*

Author Amy Tan has endured even more hardships than the characters in her novels. She has suffered from the death of her father and brother from brain tumors and her best friend from a brutal murder. She was nearly killed in two car crashes. Her mother once attempted to murder her with a meat cleaver, she had a gun pointed at her during a mugging, and she nearly died in a mudslide. Recently, a case of undiagnosed Lyme disease prevented her from writing and even walking. She has found a way to accept her life.

For a while, I did think I was terribly unlucky, but when I considered it, I thought "How many people could have gone through all these bad things and not ever have anything that serious happen to them?" I must be incredibly lucky.

—*Amy Tan,* writer

Always fall in with what you're asked to accept. Take what is given, and make it over your way. My aim in life has always been to hold my own with whatever's going. Not against: with.

—**Robert Frost**, poet

Healing, for many, is a spiritual experience. By believing in God, the Supreme Being, karma, or another life force, you give yourself a source of hope. The belief that there is an end to suffering can be remarkably self-fulfilling. After all, with hope and faith, rejections do lose their sting. Addictions have been overcome. Losses are offset by gains. Life-threatening conditions do turn around. Opportunities can present themselves. Miracles do seem to happen. Believing in them helps.

BELIEVING

Man can live about forty days without food,
about three days without water,
about eight minutes without air, but only for
one second without hope.
—Anonymous

The thing always happens that you
really believe in; and the belief in a thing
makes it happen.
—Frank Lloyd Wright, *architect*

The wish for healing has always been
half of health.
—Seneca, *philosopher*

SEEK SPIRITUAL STRENGTH

Coping with a problem is much easier if you see a spiritual purpose in it. Some perceive hardship as a test of their faith or mettle. Others see it as a rite of passage, a way to deepen their faith.

My faith really has played a huge role in healing. And I don't know how people deal with the loss of a loved one or a child without faith. It hasn't been easy.
—*John Ramsey,* father of JonBenet Ramsey, child beauty pageant contestant who was murdered

Spirituality takes some of the significance off the things that are traps for people, like the material world. It lightens the load so you can face things with joy rather than fear.
—*John Travolta,* actor

Even when the plane crash happened, I wasn't mad at God. I just knew that there was a reason that I didn't know about why it happened.
—*Reba McEntire,* singer-songwriter, *on the death of her band in an airplane crash*

As a physician I've seen all sorts of unusual things. I have seen spontaneous remissions, or so-called miraculous cures. I have seen two people get exactly the same treatment for the same disease, one recovers, one doesn't. And I have become convinced over the years that healing is a spiritual experience. In fact, if you look at the word "healing" it comes from the word "holy." And healing is more than just a physical phenomenon.

—**Deepak Chopra**, medical doctor and writer

Others feel the presence of God or another force helping them get through a difficult situation.

When Jimmy passed, oh, that almost killed me. That's the hardest thing I've ever had to do . . . But because of my faith and where I have grown to, I know that this life that belongs to me or any of my brothers and sisters or my children, does not belong to me. We do not have the Master plan. People say, "Oh, he died so young." Hey, that wasn't your plan, that was His plan. Maybe he did his service. He's on about doing the next level of what Heavenly Father would have him to do. So that's how I feel about it. . . . I do have my days—you know it's a natural thing. But we can't claim to love the Lord, believe in that famous little saying, "Let go, and let God," and still worry. You can't have faith and worry. They don't go together.

—*Gladys Knight,* singer and actress, *on healing after her son's death*

✑

You're born.
You suffer. You die.
Fortunately,
there's a loophole.

—**Billy Graham**, minister

Craig Emory, a blue-collar guy in upstate New Hampshire, he didn't have a counseling environment around him, his friends don't go to therapy, it's not that kind of place. When his young son passed, he couldn't sleep that night. Early the next morning there was this light in the room, and he believed it was a miracle. Any one of his friends would have said it could have been a truck [shining its headlights into the room]. But he believed it was God telling him that his son had gone to heaven. . . . And that continues to help him.

—*Po Bronson,* journalist and author

There's hardly any news story that . . . doesn't have some spiritual or religious or faith dimension to it. I tell our young producers, if you go to a plane crash, and you meet a survivor, and you say to her, "Well, how did you get through it, madam?" And she said, "God got me through it."

Don't say, "Well, I understand that, madam, but what really got you through it?"

—*Peter Jennings,* journalist and news anchor

The feeling that a higher power is guiding you can be tremendously reassuring to some.

In Jamaica, on an afternoon when the blinding midday sun had chased our shadows underfoot and the team indoors for lunch, I found my moment. I walked alone to the end of a wooden pier that reached into the cleansing blue waters. There, with only the splash of waves before me, it came. With my arms flung wide and my head thrown back, it came again and again—a scream that unfurled from the core of my being, carrying my fears, my tears and my frustrations into the wind. I asked God for mercy. Then, to order and direct my life. The moment I surrendered, peace embraced me. My healing had begun.

—*Susan Taylor,* editorial director of *Essence, on overcoming her feelings of inadequacy in her career*

Spirituality doesn't have to mean belief in an organized religion. It may be developed in many different ways, including practicing yoga, reading poetry, or communing with nature.

Yoga is a spiritual practice that has incredible physical benefits. I look at it as a lifestyle, a way of living that connects me to me. You know, the word "Yoga" means union. It's like everything in Yoga yokes or unites you to something higher, the highest part of yourself. What I did for a living for so many years separated who I was from what I did, and Yoga has brought back all the parts of me. Yoga puts me in a place that is a little bit less about doing and more about being, which enables me, in fact, to do more.

—*Christy Turlington,* supermodel

If you place a fern under a stone, the next day it will be nearly invisible as if the stone has swallowed it. If you tuck the name of a loved one under your tongue too long, without speaking it it becomes blood, sigh, the little sucked in breath of air hiding everywhere beneath your words. No one sees the fuel that feeds you . . . language can carry us to understanding, and connect us to things that matter in our lives.

—*Naomi Shihab Nye,* poet and songwriter

The best remedy for those who are afraid, lonely or unhappy is to go outside, somewhere where they can be quiet, alone with the heavens, nature and God. Because only then does one feel that all is as it should be and that God wishes to see people happy, amidst the simple beauty of nature.

—**Anne Frank,** diarist and Holocaust victim

BE HOPEFUL

Have faith that some good can come out of your situation. Could it bring you closer to loved ones? Could it trigger a much-needed change of lifestyle or take you down a new and unexpected path?

I deeply believe in one's own positive will to overcome even the most daunting challenges.
—*Farrah Fawcett,* actress, *on healing after treatment for rectal cancer*

I've always been a positive person, an optimist. When I see a problem, I always say, "This can be fixed!" I always think that disastrous situations bring about the positive of great opportunities to turn things around.
—*Arnold Schwarzenegger,* actor and governor of California

Become a possibilitarian. No matter how dark things seem to be or actually are, raise your sights and see possibilities—always see them, for they're always there.
—*Norman Vincent Peale,* preacher

If we didn't have faith and the promise of a better future for ourselves and our children, we wouldn't put ourselves through the hard work and pain involved in recovery. But as time passes, we may grow discouraged at the length of the process. We may have our spirits dampened by the ups and downs along the road, feeling our faith ebb more than flow. Some people report instant release from their addictions, but for most of us it will take faith and patience to inherit the promise of a new life.

—*William Cope Moyers,* journalist, *on surviving drug and alcohol addiction and skin cancer*

Hunter Adams, the unconventional medical doctor who inspired the movie *Patch Adams*, starring Robin Williams, believes that healing is believing there will be an end to suffering, and that it's his job as a healer to inspire hope.

It's my life to inspire people. I like to see it as a river. I jumped into the river of love and fun and life as a celebration and a concern for the world, the river of hope. Most people went for a swim in the river of hope and then went and dried off. The river's current was too strong or not strong enough. I encourage them to put their trunks on and jump back in. I'm a seducer, I give them paradise and the hope that paradise is possible now. I use theatre and poetry and humour . . .

—**Hunter "Patch" Adams,** medical doctor, founder of the Gesundheit Institute, social activist, and professional clown

Believing in the best outcome can only help the healing process. Try to be optimistic. Attitude influences outcome.

My only way to survive [the car accident] was only to think positively. I could not think negatively. Because I knew I wouldn't survive if I did. You're gonna have these thoughts [though], it's only natural. Especially being a mother. Your mother will tell you. You have this incredible imagination of [bad] things that can happen. But I go, let me imagine good things. Let me imagine the opposite. Let me imagine good things happen. Can't hurt.

—**Gloria Estefan,** singer–songwriter, *on healing from a car accident that broke her back and left her temporarily paralyzed*

If children have the ability to ignore all odds and percentages, then maybe we can all learn from them. When you think about it, what other choice is there but to hope? We have two options, medically and emotionally: give up, or fight like hell.

—**Lance Armstrong**, cyclist and seven-time winner of the Tour de France, *on surviving testicular cancer*

While we don't understand the exact mechanism, we know that optimistic people have greater longevity. In one study done in Great Britain, for example, 69 women who had mastectomies were interviewed after surgery. They were divided into those who were optimistic, upbeat, and determined to conquer the cancer and those who were stoic and felt helpless about it. After five years, 75 percent of the pessimists had died, while less than half the optimists had died . . . .There's no question that your attitude affects your health.

—*Alan Loy McGinnis,* psychotherapist

The degree to which you think that something is fortunate or not is the degree to which you generate alternatives that are better or worse. Unlucky people say, "I can't believe I've been in another car accident." Lucky people go, "Wonderful. Yes, I had a car accident, but I wasn't killed. And I met the guy in the other car, and we got on really well, and there might be a relationship there."

—*Richard Wiseman,* psychologist

I think there is a faith in things and in life being a miracle. When it's tough times, you sort of know there's a good chance that it will come good. . . . I'm a bit of a fighter that way. Where I think some other people aren't as fortunate and might just think, "That's it. I'm gone."

—*Sir Paul McCartney,* singer-songwriter and widower

✐

If you realized how powerful your thoughts are, you would never think a negative thought.

—*Mildred Lisette Norman, (Peace Pilgrim),* spiritual leader and activist

✐

The reason for optimism lies in the biological fact that it keeps you happy and busy, whereas pessimism just leads to lying around and bitching. I'd rather keep happy and busy than lie around bitching, but I know this will not convince those who really like lying around and bitching. As Nietzsche said that optimism and good health always go together, and so do pessimism and morbidity, in the medical sense of the word.

—*Robert Anton Wilson,* philosopher and psychologist

Miracles happen every day. Not just in remote country villages or at holy sites halfway across the globe, but here, in our own lives.

—**Deepak Chopra**, medical doctor and writer

Healing can be life-changing. True, you may never be the same after experiencing a setback, but that isn't necessarily a bad thing. In fact, the change may be good. Think of your setback as an opportunity to make improvements in yourself. It might force you to examine your life and make major changes that you otherwise wouldn't make. May your healing be regenerative. Let it make you better than you were before.

CHANGING

*Deep unspeakable suffering may well
be called a baptism, a regeneration,
the initiation into a new state.*
—George Elliot, *writer*

∽

*My father died when I was 6 and we were
really sad, so I put on a show for my mum.
Looking back now, it was a kind of therapy.*
—Tracey Ullman, *comedian and actress*

∽

*Without fear and illness, I could
never have accomplished all I have.*
—Edvard Munch, *artist*

∽

TURN BAD EXPERIENCES AROUND

Let the healing process become a means of self-wisdom.

Human beings have the awesome ability to take any experience of their lives and create a meaning that disempowers them or one that can literally save their lives.

—*Tony Robbins,* life coach and motivational speaker

[My therapist] takes a piece of paper and a pen and makes a drawing. "Think of a puzzle," she says. She draws a square and then inside of this she adds squiggly puzzle shapes with one missing piece. "So this piece here is you." She draws an individual puzzle piece. "In recovery, your shape changes. In order for you to fit back into the rest of the puzzle, your life, the other pieces of the puzzle must also change their shapes to accommodate you."

I have the distinct feeling this will not happen. That I will end up the misplaced puzzle piece, lost under the sofa. "And if the other pieces of the puzzle don't change? What then?"

"Then," she says, "you find another puzzle to belong to."

—*Augusten Burroughs,* author of *Running with Scissors* and *Dry, on his battle with alcohol addiction*

❦

There is deep joy in discovering that you can be sick and also happy. I look for the blessings and lessons in my illness, and trust that my soul is being formed.

—*Rebecca Wells,* actress and author, *on coping with severe Lyme disease*

Is there any lesson you can extract from your hardship? Many people, in retrospect, say that surviving setbacks has given them strength and character.

I guess the universe wanted me to slow down for a minute.

—*Madonna,* singer–songwriter and actress, *on recovering from multiple fractures after falling off her horse*

❦

I think sometimes, in my younger years, I gave in to being flippant, to shooting from the hip, to overplaying the theatrics and not the issues. And I think that's one of the things I reflected about in the hospital, after my stabbing, that I should discipline myself.

—*Al Sharpton,* minister and politician, *on healing after an assassination attempt*

I do not believe that sheer suffering teaches. If suffering alone taught, all the world would be wise, since everyone suffers. To suffering must be added mourning, understanding, patience, love, openness, and a willingness to remain vulnerable.

—*Anne Morrow Lindbergh,* widow of aviator Charles Lindbergh and author, *whose son was kidnapped and murdered*

I couldn't move my legs even a millimeter. It was so painful. And it was amazing, because really, it made me appreciate every little thing. I felt like a newborn baby, learning how to sit down, how to stand up, how to walk. And I took a shower after 25 days. It was one of the most amazing moments. And it just really makes you appreciate how lucky we are. And it was—it was great.

—**Petra Nemcova,** supermodel, *on recovering from a shattered pelvis and the death of her boyfriend in the 2004 Asian Tsunami*

I consider myself actually lucky to have had [a near-death] experience, because I see a lot of people waste their lives, and a great, great friend of mine was Christopher Reeve, and we used to share this experience, and what a gift it was, in a way, to have had something traumatic happen because you then had these amazing opportunities that came your way because there were, you know, no barriers. There was no kind of, oh, you can't do this because you're not supposed to do that, or you might not be good enough, or someone might think it's not a good idea. You just go, why not? Let's try it.

—**Jane Seymour,** actress, *on experiencing a near-death experience after an allergic reaction to penicillin*

After the accident, the doctors thought I was dead and when I survived, the entertainment community thought I would never return. . . .

Funny thing is, I have returned. My personal experience, however, has changed my views in certain ways. In my previous films, death has been an answer for the characters. They were looking for the right way to die. In [the next] film, although they choose to live, the characters haven't found an answer; living is in some ways the harder choice.

—*Takeshi Kitano,* comedian, actor, and film director, *on an accident that left him partially paralyzed*

Cancer was going to be my blessing. . . . I'm just different now. I look at everybody differently. I look at every child differently. I look at every flower differently. I'm grateful for every day. It's a cliché, I know, but it really is true because once you've had a serious scare in your life it's like before and after. Once you've had it, you just appreciate everything.

—**Suzanne Somers,** actress, on healing after breast cancer

Steve Jobs, cofounder of Apple Inc., was diagnosed with a rare form of pancreatic cancer. Having survived it, he decided to change the way he lives his life.

Remembering that I'll be dead soon is the most important tool I've ever encountered to help me make the big choices in life. Because almost everything—all external expectations, all pride, all fear of embarrassment or failure—these things just fall away in the face of death, leaving only what is truly important. Remembering that you are going to die is the best way I know to avoid the trap of thinking you have something to lose. You are already naked. There is no reason not to follow your heart.

—*Steve Jobs,* cofounder and CEO of Apple Inc., *on surviving pancreatic cancer*

All the adversity I've had in my life, all my troubles and obstacles, have strengthened me . . . You may not realize it when it happens, but a kick in the teeth may be the best thing in the world for you.

—**Walt Disney**, film producer, director, animator, entrepreneur and founder of the Walt Disney Company

Many people who survived a difficult childhood believe that healing from their hardship has made them stronger as adults.

Growing up in the neighborhoods that I grew up in and having a mother who was addicted to heroin, I had to learn to be a spiritual, emotional, intellectual, and physical fighter at a young age. And it just prepared me for the struggle. Nobody was going to stop me. So by the time I got to L.A., I was fearless. And I just kept that mentality, like I'm going to get mine no matter what.

—*Jada Pinkett-Smith,* actress and singer, *on overcoming child abuse*

I'm grateful for the hungry days and the cold nights. I'm grateful for the abuse, the rejection. . . . Well, I'm grateful because it showed me how not to be. It gave me an opportunity to do something different. . . . I've experienced it on both sides. I've been rejected. I've been abandoned. I've been abused. So when there's an opportunity for me to choose another way and to be another way, to be gentler, to be kinder, I do take that opportunity. And had I not experienced that as a child, I don't know how many of those opportunities that I would have overlooked. . . .

—*Iyanla Vanzant,* speaker and spiritual healer, *on overcoming child abuse*

Actress Kathleen Turner reinvented herself during a period in her life when her father died and she and her family were virtually homeless.

Suddenly we had no home. . . . We suddenly ended up in Missouri with my mother's parents, and I went from feeling that I had the whole world to play in to feeling that I had lost everything. So I just went onstage every night, every night, every night. I dealt with it that way.

—*Kathleen Turner,* actress, *on the death of her father when she was seventeen*

George Clooney reinvented himself as an actor after his career faltered.

Well, there was a period when I couldn't get hired. . . . So I just changed my attitude. I thought, from here on out, I cannot lose a job. I'll do whatever it takes. So I'd come in with a dog under my arm for some scene. I'd pull a champagne bottle and phone out of my jacket and do the scene. People were like, "What the fuck is that?" I just thought, Fuck it. It's where I'm going to hit the ball, not if I'm going to hit it.

—*George Clooney*, actor, *on overcoming career setbacks*

Many say that divorce, as heartbreaking as it is, is also an opportunity for people to reinvent themselves.

You get to reinvent yourself and feel like a new person and do things that maybe you couldn't do in the marriage. He didn't like to travel, let's say, and now you can finally see San Francisco. Or he didn't like to entertain, and now you get to get those dinner parties going. . . . [Y]ou get to fall in love again, and you get to figure out what was wrong with that type of person for you. And the best thing you can do, and therapy helps, is to figure out who you should marry the next time.

—*Kate White*, editor-in-chief of *Cosmopolitan* magazine, *on surviving divorce*

෴

When you get those divorce papers, you find out that you're still the same woman. Just a little free-er.

—*Patti LaBelle,* singer, *on surviving divorce*

After Magic Johnson was diagnosed with HIV, he improved his marriage. Cookie Johnson, his wife, says that every moment now is precious.

You know how little things used to bother you? Well, now it's like nothing. Things just roll off our heads, and we just keep going because there's a bigger issue up there. . . . We just have a good time every single day. . . . We talk about everything and we have never been closer. Sometimes Earvin will come home and say, "Let's get out of the house, just me and you," and he always makes sure somehow we always have time for each other.

—*Earleatha "Cookie" Johnson,* wife of basketball star Magic Johnson, *on coping with her husband's diagnosis of HIV*

When actress Elisabeth Shue's brother died tragically, she learned crucial lifelong lessons.

[My brother's] death stripped away the dishonesty in my life. I went into therapy because of it, which was the first huge step [I took] in my life. What happened to Will taught me that human beings are fragile. His death taught me not to be afraid anymore of who I was. . . . Will had loved me unconditionally for who I was, the way a lot of people in my life hadn't, which is, I think, why I tried so hard to please everybody. Once he was gone, I could see that in a major way, so I could finally get on with living my life as myself and finding those things in my life that fulfilled me, knowing that life was short.

—*Elisabeth Shue,* actress, *who witnessed the death of her older brother from an accident on a tire swing*

Even tragedies can bring out the best in people.

I think that situations like [September 11] can bring out the best in people. I have read, for example, that during the blitz in London, during World War II, that mental health was at an all-time high. The depression almost disappeared, anxiety disappeared. So in the face of that kind of threat, sometimes that can bring out the best in people.

—*Deepak Chopra,* medical doctor and writer

I have got to make everything that has happened to me good for me. The plank bed, the loathsome food, the hard ropes shredded into oakum till one's fingertips grow dull with pain, the menial offices with which each day begins and finishes, the harsh orders that routine seems to necessitate, the dreadful dress that makes sorrow grotesque to look at, the silence, the solitude, the shame—each and all of these things I have to transform into a spiritual experience. There is not a single degradation of the body which I must not try and make into a spiritualising of the soul.

—**Oscar Wilde**, playwright and writer, *on coping with his jail sentence*

BREAK BAD HABITS

Regard your setback as an opportunity to wipe clean the slate. Identify any bad habits that require correction. Check yourself.

It's always hard to recover after a loss. . . . I have to know when it's time to step up, not to revert back to bad habits but to keep ahead with the good ones.
—*Venus Williams,* tennis player

It is by going down into the abyss that we recover the treasures of life. Where you stumble, there lies your treasure.
—*Joseph Campbell,* writer and orator

You might consider your setback a "wake-up call" of sorts—a warning that you need to make changes in your life.

Nothing so needs reforming as other people's habits.
—*Mark Twain,* writer and humorist

[I got depressed because] I had basically taken on too much work. I have pushed the boat out as far as I should in terms of taking on too many things. I'm getting older and I just could not take it any more. I am now monitoring myself very closely and I'm just trying not to get into that sort of state again. It was as if I had been in the fast lane without bothering to change oil and with my foot on the accelerator permanently. I was just belting along and various gaskets had to get worn eventually. You convince yourself that you're happy. You say: "I can't be miserable because I'm supposedly successful." But happiness is no respecter of persons.

—*Stephen Fry,* comedian, writer, and actor, *on recovering from depression*

Be open to developing new, better habits, especially in regard to your attitude toward change. Tap into your emotions. Become more open to possibility. As with the body, permanent mental flexibility is a lifelong exercise.

I worry very much that we are inclined to fall into habits, to set shells of protection around ourselves to stop real emotions from getting through. It's necessary to keep that openness throughout life. People turn out to be so rigid that they actually snap when a trauma arrives. It's a joke, isn't it, the mid-life crisis? And it's because people have spent 20 years pushing away all the big emotions, all the real feelings. Then, suddenly, those things just come back at you with all the force accumulated over those years.

—*Jeanette Winterson,* writer

Great is the power of habit. It teaches us to bear fatigue and to despise wounds and pain.

—*Marcus Tullius Cicero,* lawyer, orator, and scholar

BECOME SOMEONE BETTER

Many people become more philosophical, spiritual, and focused when they rebound from a major setback.

If it were possible for us to see further than our knowledge extends and out a little over the outworks of our surmising, perhaps we should then bear our sorrows with greater confidence than our joys. For they are the moments when something new, something unknown, has entered into us. The more patient, quiet and open we are in our sorrowing, the more deeply and the more unhesitatingly will the new thing enter us, the better shall we deserve it, the more will it be our own destiny.

—**Rainer Maria Rilke**, poet

⁓

Illness, loss of loved ones, disappointment, decline, death, limitations, and imperfections startle and shake us. But they awaken us to find meaning, dignity, and significance in our lives . . . .It is through suffering and pain that we break down our habitual barriers between ourselves and others and allow for the entrance of a transpersonal, transcendent perspective: a full appreciation of our intimate and profound spiritual connections.

—*Kathleen Brehony,* psychologist and personal coach

Everything changes. What [the Dalai Lama] is going through at that moment—his suffering and the suffering of his people—is ultimately the shape of all things. It's a reminder that we all have to overcome the moment of truth in the moment of death, which is the ultimate reality; it gives us an awareness of where we fit in in the universe. Life is just straggling toward that.

—*Martin Scorsese,* filmmaker

Connecting with other people
is an effective way to overcome grief, anxiety, sickness, or denial. Those suffering from medical conditions often find courage by talking to others who have similar conditions. Parents often find the strength to overcome their problems by focusing on their children's happiness. Those who are depressed or have addictions may heal by talking to friends, loved ones, or mental health professionals about their issues. The comfort of knowing you're not alone is in itself remarkably healing.

CONNECTING

*I have a couple of girlfriends who are
healing. We take care of each other.
They know when I need to be taken care of.*
—**Maggie Gyllenhaal**, *actress*

*Words of comfort, skillfully administered,
are the oldest therapy known to man.*
—**Louis Nizer**, *lawyer*

*I don't want to hold anything in so
it festers and turns into pus—
a pustule of emotion that explodes into
a festering cesspool of depression.*
—**Nicolas Cage**, *actor*

FIND COURAGE THROUGH OTHERS

Seek out those who are going through similar experiences. Remember that you are not alone in your pain. Your compassion, and theirs, will strengthen you.

Healing yourself is connected with healing others.
—*Yoko Ono,* musician, *on healing after her husband John Lennon was murdered*

My mother went through a concentration camp experience. She was in Indonesia and Japanese in World War II. And she said to me, the only reason that she survived as opposed to a lot of other people who didn't survive, was that she decided to nurse, to take care of other people there. And so what she said, is she took herself out of herself. Rather than saying, why me, I can't handle this. I can't do this anymore. She just went—she said to me, always—there's always someone worse off than you. There's always someone that has a much harder situation than you have.
—*Jane Seymour,* actress

Shift your focus from yourself to others.

People hang on to their pain no matter how hard it is until they find something they value more. I dealt with a few people who have lost family members [at the World Trade Center on 9/11]. And one of the ways to get them to make that change is not to negate the experience, because they have to go through the emotions of shock and denial and hurt and anger, but eventually acceptance, and then they have to take some kind of action to honor those people that have passed on. And if they can find higher meaning, like for example they have a son that they still need to take care of, out of our need to serve others we care about, we will rise to that higher occasion. . . .

—*Tony Robbins,* coach and motivational speaker, *on healing after the September 11 terrorist attacks*

&

I have a picture I keep in my Bible, and it's of a 45-year-old man who had a stroke, and his wife dressed him all up in a suit. And he's sitting in a wheelchair, and in the wheelchair, he's all bent over like this, and she took his little black dog and she sat his little dog in his lap. He loved that little dog. He didn't even know that little dog was there. But here sits that little dog, and the man in the wheelchair has to have everything done for him, can't lift his arms, can't walk, can't speak, can't do anything.

And here I am. I can walk around New York. I can talk. I can do my own hair, put my eyelashes on. I can jump out of bed in the morning. Sure, I might feel sick to my stomach. Sure, I might feel really tired, but at least I can walk and I can talk, and I can be a part of the world.

And I said, God, if you're going to heal anybody, if you're going to give anybody a miracle . . . give this young man a miracle. He's the one that deserves it.
—*Tammy Faye Messner,* singer, TV host, and evangelist, *on healing from lung cancer*

You will discover that you have two hands. One is for helping yourself and the other is for helping others.
—*Audrey Hepburn,* actress

Being with my Mother in her last days helped me move out of the breakdown. Because I had focused on someone else. I started doing volunteer work with people who are making their transition. Not hospice work, this took place through a church that I worked through. They'd send me out to people that had asked for support. It kept me very grounded and humble. I felt like my only job was to "hold a good space" for them to die in, for them, whatever they thought that was, without imposing my ideas on them. I learned it wasn't my concept of they way they should die, but their idea of how they wanted to go, their wish for their environment. Some people wanted to talk. Some wanted to know what I thought was next. Sometimes it was folding socks and putting them in a drawer: keeping it very light.
—**David Allen Brooks,** actor, *on recovering from a nervous breakdown*

∽

It is one of the most beautiful compensations of life, that no man can sincerely try to help another without helping himself.
—**Ralph Waldo Emerson,** writer and poet

∽

I remember when I finally made the choice [to sing at the Grammy Awards]. Yeah, I'm going to do it bald. And you know what? Maybe this'll help somebody who's on chemo lying in bed and going, God, I'm bald. Isn't this weird? Maybe it'll help them feel a little better.

—*Melissa Etheridge,* singer-songwriter, *on healing after breast cancer*

By connecting to others and having compassion for them, you displace your own fears and insecurities.

My left arm is half the size of my right. It's about three inches shorter. I've learned to carry it so that it doesn't look that way. When I was in New York, I decided to have it fixed. I went to a clubfoot clinic in New York Hospital. . . . I was the first one there. Soon the room filled up with people who were really suffering. I got up and left. I said, "I don't have a problem. These guys are the ones who have real problems."

—*Martin Sheen,* actor

∽

The death of a loved one is often an incentive to improve oneself on the behalf of that person. It's a way of healing from that loss.

When [my mother] passed away, I kind of understood the commitment that she made to make sure that I could stay in skating. And I wanted to live up to whatever I could. Not so much win everything, but just to be the best that I could possibly be, to honor her memory and everything she went through to make sure that I was given the opportunities to be the best that I can be. Not to be a world champion or an Olympic gold medalist, but to be the best that I could be. And that was the most important thing that ever happened in my career.

—*Scott Hamilton,* Olympic skater and testicular cancer survivor

There's a story in [my book] from a woman in Minneapolis, and she was married for 43 years and she had six sons with her husband. And they travelled a lot, they moved around a lot because of his job. And every time they moved it was hard on her. And when she'd be kind of down about it, her husband would say, "Oh, don't worry honey, you're just getting started." And when one of the boys would make the baseball team he'd say, "Hey, look at you, you're just getting started." And then when they didn't, he'd say—when they didn't make the team, he'd say, "Oh, well don't worry, you're just getting started." Anyway, he died, and she was devastated. I mean, this was her lover, her best friend, and for months she was in a very blue place. And she said one morning she woke up, and she hears this little voice in her head, and it said, "Don't worry, honey, you're just getting started." So moving to me, that story.

—*Marlo Thomas,* actress

Many people look to their children as a source of strength and conviction to make it through a tough time.

I found courage looking into the eyes of my children: my beautiful daughter—she's 18 years old now—and my son. I look at them and know I have a reason to live. Now my son's father and I are friends. We're close. There's a lot of love between us and always will be. We know we're bound by God to do right by our child. And we will. But the breakup was hard, and there are no magic tricks for getting through the pain. Only time.

—*Angie Stone,* singer-songwriter, *on healing a broken heart*

We all face our own mortality every day, but we aren't forced to think about it. I'm forced to face it. I don't want [my son] Dylan to see me afraid. I don't mind him seeing me sad. I don't mind him seeing me cry. But I don't want him to see me afraid.

—**Joel Siegel**, film critic, on coping with colon cancer

I had NO IDEA that mothering my own child would be so healing to my own sadness from my childhood. Doing the right thing for someone else was like a tonic for me; it was like some magic ointment that made a wound disappear.

—*Susie Bright,* performance artist

Being with [my son] Kai I could start to see the things that kept me from really being present and really living my life. It's made me more available as a person, which affects what I can give to my work. It's made me aware of things that I wasn't aware of before—in myself and in the world. I've always been looking for something sacred in my life: I've always read religious texts and philosophy and I've found what I've been looking for in a much more practical way—in the process of living life.

—*Jennifer Connelly,* actress

TALK ABOUT IT

The healing process works when you talk about your situation. It allows you to express and articulate your fears, which may help you control them better. And it gives others a chance to understand what you're going through.

I think that people heal their war wounds when they are able to communicate in story. When we tell one another our stories, people can help us carry our burdens.
—*Maxine Hong Kingston,* writer

❧

Nobody ever talked to me when my mother got cancer. Nobody sat me down to tell me about her condition, that she would be okay or what would happen if she wasn't. [When my husband got cancer] I sat my kids down. It was a great time for me to learn how to communicate with them that things would be okay, regardless. "Even if your dad dies, it'll be alright. We'll survive. We'll get through this. We'll send a lot of love and do the best we can to help dad help himself."
—*Mariel Hemingway*, actress, *on coping with cancer in her family*

❧

Stay communicating with the people around you. Everyone gets overwhelmed at points, but it's when you think you can handle it yourself and you don't reach out for help—that's when the end is near. Recognize that you are about to tire, that drowning is looming.

—*Keith Urban,* singer, *on battling alcohol addiction*

✍

It has taken the whole three years [after our son's death] for [our family] . . . to rebuild ourselves. And during that period of rebuilding ourselves, we learned to communicate differently with one another. . . . We learned to not rush through things as we talk to one another. To say what we really mean. To spend more time with one another. To show our appreciation for one another. Not to just rush through a day and take it for granted that a person will be around, because that might not be true.

—*Camille Cosby,* producer and wife of comedian Bill Cosby, *on healing after the death of her son who was shot on the LA thruway in a random act of violence*

✍

I never used to open up to people about my problems. I always felt like I had to be the survivor, I had to be the strong one, the tough one. I had to be—you know, everyone else's caretaker. Through my therapy—and I didn't reach out to anybody after the rape, and after my separation from [my husband] and through the therapy I realized that to be a whole person and a well-rounded person you have to take as well as give, otherwise you end up emotionally bankrupt eventually.

—**Fran Drescher,** actress, *on surviving rape, divorce, and uterine cancer*

When I was 12 years old, I had a mental break-down; I went berserk for a long time. I felt rejection from the white community. Couldn't understand why the pigmentation of my skin kept me from doing. . . . The breakdown was very vivid. I just all of a sudden felt like I had been overcome by a train. . . . Within three months I began to heal. And the healing came about through community, again. When I would get up at nighttime and start walking the floor, either my brothers, my sister, my mother, my father, or members of the community would come in and pace the floor with me. They would just say, "It's nothing there." And I'd say, "Oh, yes there are. They're coming to get me. They're coming to get me." Very paranoid. And they would say, "But we love you. We're going to stay with you. Don't you worry." And they would rock me and touch me and embrace me, and it was an incredible experience.

—*Cecil Williams,* minister, *on recovering from a childhood mental breakdown*

ASK FOR HELP

Even the people closest to you may not realize when you need help. It may be difficult to explicitly ask for someone's help in working through your problem, but it may help you heal.

I inherited the disease of alcoholism, and I learned early to get help when I needed it. I always went to people who knew more than I did.
—*Liza Minnelli,* actress, *on surviving alcohol addiction*

[When you get] a splinter in your finger it never gets well until you get it out. Whether you're a 6-year-old when you disclose or whether you're 22 years old or whether you're 35 years old it's important to be able to say "Hey, listen, I have this splinter and I need somebody to help me get it out."
—*Astrid Heger,* medical doctor, *on how to recover from childhood abuse*

Choose that person carefully. Each of us instinctively knows the type of care we require, and who would be able to deliver it at a time of need.

When we honestly ask ourselves which person in our lives means the most to us, we often find that it is those who, instead of giving much advice, solutions, or cures, have chosen rather to share our pain and touch our wounds with a gentle and tender hand. The friend who can be silent with us in a moment of despair or confusion, who can stay with us in an hour of grief and bereavement, who can tolerate not knowing, not curing, not healing and face with us the reality of our powerlessness, that is a friend who cares.

—*Henri Nouwen,* priest and writer

❧

"What's wrong?" "Why don't you get out and do something?" "You'd feel better if you got up and took a shower." . . . When I've started down that long black spiral into depression, such well-intentioned comments are more hurtful than helpful. The first two simply have no answer, and all three require answers or action of which I'm incapable and thus feed my feeling of hopelessness. The words that are most welcome are "What can I do to help?" Sometimes I need a hug, or someone to do a specific task that I feel is overwhelming, or just a quiet presence in the room, someone not trying to "fix" the situation or supply answers or suggestions for improvement. Sometimes I just need someone to be there, so the dark isn't quite so big.

—*Kathy Cronkite,* journalist and public speaker, *on overcoming depression*

If you're looking to solutions and looking to what is good in your life and what is positive in your life, and you get rid of the people who are negative and dark in your life, you have a greater chance of surviving.

—*Richard Lawson,* actor, *on surviving a near-death experience in an airplane crash*

I think that when you go through something that's when you find out who your true friends are. It might be a cliché but it's so true.

—*Don Cheadle,* actor

Physical suffering aside, a healing presence can relieve emotional suffering. A case in point is a functional magnetic resonance imaging study of women awaiting an electric shock. When the women endured their apprehension alone, activity in neural regions that incite stress hormones and anxiety was heightened. As . . . reported last year in an article in Psychophysiology, *when a stranger held the subject's hand as she waited, she found little relief. When her husband held her hand, she not only felt calm, but her brain circuitry quieted, revealing the biology of emotional rescue.*

—**Daniel Goleman**, psychologist and author

I now have to construct a new way of thinking, a new way of life, because the one I had led me to being fucking miserable. When I cleaned up, I thought, Now is the time for something to give me unconditional love, and I will give it unconditional love back, and I thought, Well, that's a dog.

—Robbie Williams, singer-songwriter, *on recovering from alcohol addiction*

BE TRUTHFUL

You may be embarrassed to show weakness. But suppressing your problems may make them worse. Others may surprise you with their understanding and compassion.

You ought to tell people right up front you've got a problem, and if it's resolved, then they don't have any doubts about it. When I made this statement about prostate cancer, I had mail coming from all over the country—hundreds and hundreds of letters when I was in the hospital. So it occurred to me (maybe you can make a plus out of a minus) to get busy and start contacting some of these people and learning more about it. . . .

—**Bob Dole,** politician, *on revealing his diagnosis of prostate cancer*

My biggest fear was really going public, because you know, we in America don't accept disease and illness very well. We look at that as being weakness, and I'm not a weak person. I'm just ill right now, and I'm going to get through it and I am going to show some of those other victims and sufferers of this dis-

ease that—you know what?—I know your
pain, I really do.

—**Montel Williams,** talk show host, *on reveal-*
ing that he has multiple sclerosis

I tell the basics [of my Parkinson's disease] in
an honest, open way and then let [my children]
be with it. What's important for them is not
how I feel about having PD, but how they feel
about my having PD. I give them reassurance,
because I'm a classic optimist, not a fearful
person, but it's their experience that matters.
It really hasn't been a big thing—they know
they can ask me anything anytime—we've got
a lot of regular everyday family stuff going on.

—**Michael J. Fox,** actor, *on revealing his diagno-*
sis of Parkinson's disease

**Revealing your problems may unexpectedly help
others through similar experiences.**

When I decided to write about my illness, I
thought to myself, everybody I loved, the people I most cared about who might be hurt by a
revelation—my friends and my family—they

already knew. I felt confident that, as Bill Murray might say, "That won't hurt ya none." I knew how the media worked and what kind of coverage it would likely get, and I knew the effect—even if short-lived—would be to address the stigma many people with mental illness face. . . . I can't say it was a decision I agonized over much, if at all. I instantly saw a unique way to redeem a really horrible situation.

—*Jane Pauley*, television anchor and journalist, *on revealing her struggle with bipolar disorder*

After nearly a year of angst, I decided to speak out publicly [about AIDS]. Since I had only a short while to live, I needed to make an impact fast. Besides, if people didn't like what I said, what could they do—kill me? So I took to the stage with the hope that a dying woman could make a difference for the living.

—*Mary Fisher*, activist and daughter of prominent Republican fundraisers, *on healing after her diagnosis of HIV transmitted to her by her late husband*

I didn't want to talk about the stigma of depression. Finally, one night I was on the Bob Costas Show, back when he did Later on television, about 1:30 in the morning. In the middle of it, I suddenly realized, "Hey, the people who are watching at this time of night are people who can't sleep." So I decided those are the people that I used to be, and that is the first time I began to go public about it. It lifted an extraordinary burden. Since that time I have talked about it fairly openly for the reason that it can be helpful for other people to say, "Well look, here's a guy who was at the bottom of the heap, miserable, and look, he has it back. He is surviving."

—**Mike Wallace,** journalist and TV correspondent, *on revealing his struggle with clinical depression*

SEEK PROFESSIONAL HELP
IF NECESSARY

Counselors, psychologists, and psychiatrists may help you in times of crisis, or as part of a long-term agenda for emotional healing. Many well-known people have benefited from professional help.

It was either therapy or die.
—*Mickey Rourke,* actor

I'm a big believer in therapy. I'm in therapy in real life. I think anytime you can bitch and moan about your own life to someone who really doesn't care that much, and can give you an objective opinion about what you're going through, I think that's valuable.
—*Eric Stoltz,* actor

Wine led to tequila, then vodka, then to drugs, which led to whatever. I don't really have a recollection of what happened after that, but I woke up in a jail cell. . . . I was panicked and confused. The police had told me that I had beaten up a girl, and that was just the worst possible thing that I could've ever heard. I was freaked out. . . . So a couple of days later, with the help of a friend, I made the decision to check into rehab and just surrender, become willing to try things a different way, because my way was winding me up in a lot of trouble.

—***Christian Slater,*** actor, *on recovering from drug and alcohol abuse*

When they'd said, "You've got to go into treatment for six weeks," I'd replied, "But I've got an album to do! I can't take six weeks off!" But the time off is what saved my life. I want to beat this self-destructive thing. It's a constant battle, but I've had treatment, I took a year off. I'd never taken a year off in my life, but learned not to run away from it now. The diseases of alcoholism and addiction are about running away from stuff.

—***Sir Elton John,*** singer and composer, *on recovering from depression and alcohol abuse*

A lot of what I've been learning in the last two years is due to therapy—about my sexuality, why things go wrong, why relationships haven't worked. It isn't anything to do with anybody else; it's to do with me. You have to confront things in yourself. I've always used various addictions to anesthetize myself—drag, drugs, fame, sex, religion, food—and there's been a lot of things in my life that I've wanted to run away from. Therapy opens up a window. You can try to close it, but the realization remains.

—**Boy George,** singer, *on recovering from various addictions*

[Anger] eats you up. It eats you up. I had a lot of help. I had a lot of therapy. . . . You can't just lay it on friends and children. You can't always unload to them . . . because they're going through their own very difficult times, too. And so I was very grateful that I didn't do the British stiff upper lip, but I went straight to a therapist. And she was wonderful and helpful, and I went for about two years.

—**Lynn Redgrave,** actress, *on surviving breast cancer*

I was fortunate enough to have a very intelligent person who knew the illness inside and out; he knew the biology and the psychology of the illness, he knew its treatment extremely well, and he was very perceptive about human nature, and knew all of the things that was making it difficult for me to accept treatment, to accept medication. I was very fortunate and actually one time a week, one hour a week under the circumstances of being so devastatingly ill, is actually not very much time against the tremendous amount of time that you spend psychotic or depressed.

—**Kay Redfield Jamison,** psychiatrist, *on healing from biopolar disorder*

❧

The great gift of human beings is that we have the power of empathy.

—**Meryl Streep,** actress

❧

For some, antidepressants have a role in the healing process, especially when emotional pain is at its most intense.

Taking medication is not an easy way out, as some would have you believe. I went through several years—and as many psychiatrists—before I settled on a doctor I could trust and a remedy that worked. . . . Once I found the right combination of meds, my mental agony subsided, and with it, much of my physical distress did, too. I felt as though a splinter had been removed from my brain, trailing with it the pain.

—*Eva Marer,* journalist, *on coping with bipolar disorder*

But many people who take medication find that the healing only begins after they stop taking it.

I took antidepressants for six months. I had to. . . . Once you go off them you can deal with it better. . . . It's important to go deeply into your emotions. You have to cry.

—*Olivia Newton John,* singer and actress, *on the loss of her boyfriend who vanished at sea*

HELP OTHERS, TOO

Be there when others need you, too, in the same way that you would want them to help you in times of need. Resist being judgmental. Ask what you can do to help.

There are many studies which show that a positive mental attitude, and social connections, being connected to people, actually reduces your risk of serious illness, and contributes to longevity. Volunteering, men and women who volunteer, the studies show they have a much lower mortality rate. . . . And it has to do with altruism. That used to be the way you got into heaven. Now we think it's a way to achieve health.

—*Art Ulene,* medical doctor and author

I got a letter that was passed on to me two weeks after it had arrived at the show. It said, "My little boy is very ill. He knows he's dying, and the only thing he's interested in at all is Big Bird on Sesame Street. Do you think you could phone him?" I immediately called the hospital where he was, his name was Joey, and I said, "Hello, Joey. I've heard you've been a very good boy." And he said, "Is it really you,

Big Bird?" And I said, "Yes'm." And then I said, "Oscar wants to talk to you," and I began speaking in Oscar's voice. And then finally I said, "Well, Joey, I'll let you go. It's been fun to talk to you." And he says, "Thank you for calling me, Big Bird." I got a letter the very next week from his father saying Joey died one hour later and he never stopped smiling. He hadn't smiled in a whole month.

—**Carroll Spinney,** puppeteer and voice of Big Bird on *Sesame Street*

The idea is that your partner is, among other things, your resource. And you want it to be a renewable resource, you want it to be something that self-refreshes and brings new things all the time, and you can't do that if you weigh that person down with your expectations. The great thing about [my wife] Tracy is that she still surprises me, and even with all my constraining issues like Parkinson's or whatever else, I still surprise her and she'll go, I can't believe he did that. And even if it pisses her off, it's cool.

—**Michael J. Fox,** actor, *on living with Parkinson's disease*

Right from the moment of our birth, we are under the care and kindness of our parents, and then later on in our life when we are oppressed by sickness and become old, we are again dependent on the kindness of others. Since at the beginning and end of our lives we are so dependent on other's kindness, how can it be in the middle that we would neglect kindness towards others?

—**Dalai Lama**

Remember to listen. Often healing requires someone simply to listen without judgment and without offering advice.

Perhaps the most important thing we ever give each other is our attention. . . . A loving silence often has far more power to heal and to connect than the most well-intentioned words.
—*Rachel Naomi Remen,* medical doctor, activist, and survivor of Crohn's disease

I took a week's vacation the week before my dad died. And I went down there and spent an enormous amount of time with him and really sat. And we literally talked about everything. He knew what was happening. . . . He was incredibly strong and incredibly brave. But I got to sit at his bedside for hour after hour during that week, talking about him dying, talking about how it affected him, what his fears were, talking about my childhood and our early days together. I had a conversation with him on a Sunday morning, where I literally got to say good bye. I got on a plane, went back to work Monday. He died Tuesday.
—*Matt Lauer,* television host, *on healing after his father's death*

For many, complete healing means helping prevent whatever happened to you from happening to others.

I think of women and men across the planet, who have been through terrible violence, terrible pain, and rather than getting an AK-47 or retaliating or becoming avengers or revengers, they actually grieve what happened to them, they experience what happened to them, and in doing that something transforms them and they then commit their lives to making sure it doesn't happen to anyone else. . . . When you give what you need the most, you heal whatever is broken. What we are waiting for has always lived inside us. I think what I would say to anyone is—stop waiting. Stop retaliating. Stop living your life as if you're going to be rescued, and give what you need the most. And you will heal and you will transform whatever pain is inside you.
—*Eve Ensler,* playwright, *on healing from childhood sexual abuse*

It's a really tragic thing when you have experienced breast cancer. The death of a loved one when it is seemingly unnecessary is very, very painful. The only positive thing you can really gain through losing someone is learning, and teaching other people. So I hope to teach other people, and I hope to learn.

—*Stella McCartney,* fashion designer and cancer education advocate, *on healing after her mother, Linda McCartney, died of breast cancer*

ACKNOWLEDGE THOSE WHO HELP YOU

Acknowledging others for their role in your life will empower them as much as they've empowered you. It's a virtuous cycle.

Sharon saved my life every day. I mean to say, "I love my wife" is not enough. I absolutely live for my wife. Last year looking back, I imploded emotionally. I couldn't speak, I couldn't walk— literally. My speech is only now beginning.

—*Ozzy Osbourne,* singer-songwriter, *on recovering from alcohol and drug addiction*

On particularly dark days, I'd be lying on the bathroom floor wailing and [my boyfriend] would say, "OK, honey, you can cry for just five minutes, then I'm taking you on the bike for a ride around Paris." . . . I'd find myself thinking, "Hmm. Actually a ride on the bike sounds pretty good."

—*Kylie Minogue,* singer-songwriter, *on surviving breast cancer*

John was always there by my side. I cannot say enough about what a great husband he has been through all of this. John and I are so completely connected. There is nothing closer than where we are now.

—*Elizabeth Edwards,* former attorney and wife of presidential candidate John Edwards, *on her battle against breast cancer and the death of their son in a car accident*

I had the most amazing ultrasound doctor. . . . She looked at me and said, "Melissa, whatever this is, whatever road you have to go down, believe me, you will be fine. I was diagnosed five years ago, and I am fine." And she had a full mastectomy. And she opened up and said, "This is the worst that can happen to you." It really set me on the road. And I kept that in my mind, "I will be fine."

—**Melissa Etheridge,** singer-songwriter, *on surviving breast cancer*

∞

[After my diagnosis] people I hadn't seen in years sent their best and, as crass as it sounds, all the messages of support I had here . . . genuinely made a difference. I always used to think these things were a waste of time and kind of scoffed at strangers doing this kind of thing. But it really does help. When you're feeling like shit, there's honestly nothing nicer than pages and pages of people wishing you the best.

—**Mark Millar,** cartoonist and illustrator, *on coping with Crohn's disease*

∞

When I had my birthday party in February—it was a nice dinner, about fifteen of us—I looked around the table and I said to myself, "I can't believe that I'm so lucky to be surrounded by these people right now. I'm twenty years old today. I've carried myself through the years. I've made mistakes along the way, but they were the kind of mistakes that we all have to make in order to learn." And, thank God, I did learn. . . . To me, that moment on that day was like a version of my favorite game, Dog Out the Window. . . . It's when you put your head out the window and you let the wind rush at you. And that's what it was like—it was a rush . . . .

—**Drew Barrymore,** actress and film producer, *on overcoming drug and alcohol addiction*

The power of love to change bodies is legendary, built into folklore, common sense, and everyday experience. Love moves the flesh, it pushes matter around. . . . Throughout history, "tender loving care" has uniformly been recognized as a valuable element in healing.

—**Larry Dossey,** medical doctor

At times our own light goes out and is rekindled by a spark from another person. Each of us has cause to think with deep gratitude of those who have lighted the flame within us.

—**Albert Schweitzer,** theologian, philosopher, and medical doctor

Many people who are undergoing difficult times in their lives decide to channel their pain into something productive: art, writing, music, public speaking, and so on. The process of creating something is in itself life-affirming. Create something to express yourself, distract yourself, or draw attention to or from yourself. In the end, you may decide to share what you've created, which helps you reach out to others—and helps them connect to you.

CREATING

❦

I never understood death before . . .
So I decided to do a film about the culture
of death, to see if I'd made progress.
Now I can look death in the face.
—**Pedro Almodovar**, *filmmaker*

❦

Well, art is a great antibody, isn't it?
—**Patti Smith**, *singer-songwriter*

❦

I could have been in deep trauma, but when
I was playing the pipes it didn't matter.
—**Davy Spillane**, *musician*

❦

Simple and plain, rapping is good therapy.
—**Ice Cube**, *rapper*

❦

WRITE ABOUT IT

Try writing about your experience. Your writing doesn't need to be a manifesto or the Great American novel. The goal here is to work through your pain by articulating it in a safe way. Of course, you can share it if you want—you can write a best-selling autobiography on your path to recovery— but the real purpose of your writing is to help you heal.

We are healed of a suffering only by expressing it to the full.
—*Marcel Proust,* writer

Writing is such a healing thing. You simply rearrange reality. A rich interior life is a great place to go on vacation.
—*Ingrid Hill,* writer

The only time that I wasn't thinking about dealing with physical suffering is when I was working on [best-selling novel *Sea Biscuit*]. I've never been more alive as when I worked on this book.
—*Laura Hillenbrand,* writer, *on coping with chronic fatigue syndrome*

Cancer is only a word, like any other. . . . The word reverberated . . . I gripped it in my mind's fist like a hot stone, unable to throw it far from me, letting it burn into my skin. I was angry. I wanted to hit people with it. Then, the next moment I wanted to make a prayer out of it, I wanted to write a poem with it.

—**Rafael Campo**, poet and medical doctor

Writing can help you break a destructive cycle. Author Amy Tan relates how writing about how a legacy of depression and suicide in her family helped her overcome the fate of her grandmother who committed suicide.

Legacies can be fateful unless you're aware of how that stream has maintained itself. By understanding that sense of fate and writing about it, I feel that I have broken it. I feel I am conversing with my grandmother, who of course I never met. By looking at why she did this and her sense of both anger and despair in not having a voice, I'm saying to her: we have a voice now, we can give voice to this.

—*Amy Tan,* writer, *on overcoming depression*

Make a habit of writing. From an early age, many famous artists used writing as a way to deal with life's challenges.

Need actually came around the time of my parents' divorce, when I was about eight. Writing became my therapist. It made me intimate with myself. For a child, divorce is like being torn out of the only air you've ever known, and you're suddenly in a very strange climate. My pen became, to a large degree, my oxygen supply, my link to what was real and what I knew was sincere inside myself. No matter what was going on, I had something that I was relative to, that I felt safe in. I think I became oddly dependent on writing. It started to become like a third limb or a sixth sense with me.

—*Jewel,* singer-songwriter, *on recovering from her parents' divorce*

Many people write explicitly about their struggles. Governor George McGovern wrote a biography of his daughter who had committed suicide.

I wanted my daughter's life, her good points as well as her weaknesses, to be understood. I wanted people to see that this special daughter was a lot more than simply an alcoholic, so I wanted to try to present as complete as possible a picture of who Teresa Jane McGovern was and what she stood for. In that respect, it was written for her. But I also think I wrote it for myself, to see if I could come to terms with some of the regrets that I've had about my daughter, where I saw mistakes being made either by myself or by others in my daughter's life.

—*George McGovern,* governor of South Dakota and presidential nominee, *on the death of his daughter*

Telling your story can help you reposition and better understand actual events in your life. The act of reframing your experience can be healing.

. . . We ask [soldiers in the Iraq War] to tell their story. . . . We want them to get their story out. It metabolizes that experience for them. Once they get the story out to us of what happened, it helps us to reframe that story for the positive things they have said and to reinforce those positive things. And there are many positive things because they carry out their orders under extreme pressure. It sort of tells them, wow, my training kicked in here. I've done the little things I was trained to do, even with an increased heart rate and the adrenaline and perhaps chaos.

—*Rev. Maj. Malcolm Berry,* Canadian military chaplain, *on healing during wartime*

Language itself can be calming.

Repetition I love, and use it because it made me feel safe. Repeated words and phrases have a rocking feeling, like a lullaby. They help take away the shock of the plot—death, lives destroyed or the horror of the settings—a crazy, chaotic, emotional house, the sinister movie theater.

—*Arundhati Roy,* writer

Writing or reading poetry is particularly healing, for it both evokes emotions and is soothing to hear.

. . . They told us when a patient's sedated, their hearing is the last sense to go and she could probably hear my voice, even if she couldn't put together what was going on. So I basically tried to stand in her room and talk to her. When I started to find things I could read to her—and that's when I settled on poetry because it was something I could read for a long time and a friend of mine gave me a book of a "Poem a Day." And I just read to her. Sometimes I would read 50, 60 poems a day.

—*Greg Manning,* banker, *on helping his wife Lauren Manning heal after she nearly died in terrorist attacks of 9/11*

Poetry may make us from time to time a little more aware of the deeper, unnamed feelings which form the substratum of our being, to which we rarely penetrate; for our lives are mostly a constant evasion of ourselves.

—*T. S. Eliot,* poet

MAKE—OR LISTEN TO—MUSIC

Many musicians write songs to help them heal. Indeed, many famous artists say the therapeutic value of music inspired them to become musicians in the first place.

Singing becomes a form of therapy.
—*Placido Domingo,* singer

I almost subconsciously use music for myself as a healing agent, and lo and behold, it worked. Great music has always touched something in me which—absolved me from whatever—you know, the dark condition was.
—*Eric Clapton,* singer-songwriter, *on coping with the death of his infant son*

I think music in itself is healing. It's an explosive expression of humanity. It's something we are all touched by. No matter what culture we're from, everyone loves music.
—*Billy Joel,* singer-songwriter

Music reminds you about your body, but it also takes you out of it. All art is a form of escape, but music is in particular. In order to achieve a feeling of escape in my music—to feel free—I need to trap myself more and more. In a work situation, I mean. I'm sure it's like that for most artists. There's not only the desire to achieve freedom through your work but the desire to achieve the feeling that you are creating something that has never existed. There are many types of power, but the power to create is the ultimate one.

—**Laurie Anderson,** performance artist and musician

Musicians say that making music helps them turn negative emotions into positive, productive ones.

The great thing about being able to create and make music is that you can take things that have been hurtful to you and you can release those emotions and make them into songs. And even if it is a sad song it is like you have taken an experience, and you have used it, and you have turned it into something that is ultimately helping you. Because just the act of singing words that you write down that are therapeutic for you is something that is very healing, and it is also great because you can inspire other people who listen to this music.

—*Mariah Carey,* singer-songwriter

✆

This whole record [Matchbox Twenty's Platinum-winning *Something to Be*] was kind of made under duress. The entire time I was working on it, my wife was really sick, and dealing with that made the record itself not the most important thing in my life. It was good in that way because I completely trusted my instincts. I would just come into the studio, and if a song sounded really good, I would just walk away from it so I could get home to whatever was going on. . . . "Now Comes the Night" is about death and being less scared to face it with someone by your side. . . . And I get the added bonus of going out and screaming the lyrics, which feels so good, man. You know, not a lot of people get paid to go through primal scream therapy.

—*Rob Thomas,* singer-songwriter, *on coping with his wife's rare autoimmune disorder*

At the very least, songwriting may be a way to deal with complex emotions.

I have written a song that says: If you ever lose someone dear to you, never say the words, "They're gone," and they'll come back.

—*Prince,* singer-songwriter, *on the death of his infant son*

["Me and a Gun" is] a song about brutality and invasion on the deepest level. . . . To heal the wound you have to go into the dark night of the soul.

—Tori Amos, singer-songwriter, on the lyrics to a song she wrote after she was kidnapped and raped in her early twenties

EXPRESS YOURSELF IN ART

Drawing, sketching, and painting are other ways to express your fears, needs, visions, dilemmas.

In today's climate in our country, which is sickened with the pollution of pollution, threatened with the prominence of AIDS, riddled with burgeoning racism, rife with growing huddles of the homeless, we need art and we need art in all forms. We need all methods of art to be present, everywhere present, and all the time present.

—*Maya Angelou,* poet and Pulitzer prize winner

Art and music are very healing to me. I think they're two of the most powerful healing forces in the universe. I mean, have you ever gone to a museum and stood in front of a Vermeer and just had tears roll down your cheeks? That doesn't happen when people stand in front of First National Bank.

—*Roseanne Cash,* singer-songwriter

Out of many terrible things that happened, instead of falling into major depression or bankruptcy I wound up with the greatest gifts in my life. The ability to paint.

—*Jane Seymour,* actress, *on overcoming depression, marital infidelity, a near-death experience, and the death of close friends*

You know, if there's a cat, I obliterate it by putting polka dot stickers on it. I obliterate a horse by putting polka dot stickers on it. And I obliterated myself by putting the same polka dot stickers on myself. . . . I hated myself. But I was truly healed by the art I was making. Art enabled me to open up my heart, to face my own difficult character.

—*Yayoi Kusama,* artist, *on healing from child abuse*

As soon as they saw the paper and crayons coming, we couldn't get it out fast enough. And we told them to draw about the tsunami.

—*Connie Sellecca,* actress, *on helping children heal after the tsunami of 2004*

The pain passes,
but the beauty remains.

—Pierre-Auguste Renoir,
painter

Reach out to others through your art.

[Painter Jean-Michel Basquiat] smashed his head against the bars in the cell and his crown made the most beautiful sound anyone's ever heard. You could hear the ringing for miles. It was so beautiful that people wanted to grab the air, but they didn't know where the sound was coming from. That's the sound Jean-Michel made. He never got out of that cell, because I think he was in an incredible amount of pain and he felt very isolated, but the sound that he made—the art that he made—reached out to a lot of people.
—*Julian Schnabel,* artist and filmmaker, *on Basquiat coping with depression and addiction through painting*

[Through artistic expression] somebody at least for a moment feels about something or sees something the way that I do. It doesn't happen all the time. It's these brief flashes or flames, but I get that sometimes. I feel unalone—intellectually, emotionally, spiritually. I feel that I'm in a deep, significant conversation with another consciousness in fiction and poetry in a way that I don't with other art.
—*David Foster Wallace,* writer

In fact, any activity from woodworking to origami can be healing. Your creation may explicitly address the problem you're working through, or it may be completely unrelated. The creative process in itself provides an alternative reality of which you can be proud and in which you can take refuge.

My ideal relaxation is working on upholstery. I spend hours in junk shops buying furniture. I do all the upholstery work myself, and it's like therapy.

—*Pamela Anderson,* actress and model, *on recovering from divorce*

ༀ

Creativity creates energy, and energy stimulates the feeling of life. . . . I only feel my real age when I've finished one film without having started another. . . . Then remorse, doubts, and dark presentiments overwhelm me. . . .

—*Federico Fellini,* filmmaker

ༀ

For some reason I ended up a total artist dreamer and only able to cope with life through my work. My work was strong, but the rest of me was very, very weak. I am a slightly more balanced person now that I've gotten older, but when I was young, without the drawing I'm sure I would be dead.

—**R. Crumb,** artist and illustrator, *who, in his childhood, suffered from an abusive father and social rejection*

Everybody is sort of kicking me. But, I have a record and I'm going to work, so fuck it. That's the thing I have in my pocket the whole time. If I didn't have that, I'd be dead.

—**Courtney Love,** singer-songwriter, *on coping with drug and alcohol addiction and life after the death of husband, singer Kurt Cobain*

I think with Dad being gone—and me spending a lot of time in my room on my own, just drawing and painting and singing and creating an imaginary world that was in some ways more enjoyable than this responsibility that I had, something else was created.

—**Guy Pearce,** actor, *on recovering after the death of his father, a test pilot whose plane crashed when Pearce was eight*

You can be creative without being an artist. For example, a breast cancer survivor has thought up an entirely new creation: healing gardens.

Suppose there were 6,000 different trees and different species and different genuses and you went into this forest. . . . And each [tree] bore a name, you know, just as you would in an arboretum and you would have like this person was this person and that person was that person and this person was that person, and that person would go on living and that person would keep growing and you could see how the tree was doing and tie a little ribbon on it if you wanted, just whatever it was that was in your soul. That's a garden to me.

—*Topher Delaney*, artist and landscape designer, *on healing from breast cancer and the death of her father*

A garden is the best alternative therapy.
—*Germaine Greer*, writer and feminist

In my forty years as a rabbi, I have tended to many people in the last moments of their lives. Most of them were not afraid of dying. Some were old and felt that they had lived long, satisfying lives. Others were so sick and in such pain that only death would release them. The people who had the most trouble with death were those who felt that they had never done anything worthwhile in their lives, and if God would only give them another two or three years, maybe they would finally get it right. It was not death that frightened them; it was insignificance, the fear that they would die and leave no mark on the world.

—Harold Kushner, rabbi

Healing often involves over-coming some degree of resentment. It's tempting to bear a grudge against whomever or whatever you think compromised your happiness in the first place. But resentment festers and is as unhealthy as an open wound. Survivors know the best thing is to let go, as hard as it seems. Forgiveness—of others, fate, and even yourself—is crucial.

FORGIVING

❧

*The practice of forgiveness is
our most important contribution to
the healing of the world.*
—Marianne Williamson,
spiritual activist and lecturer

❧

*For every minute you remain angry, you
give up sixty seconds of peace of mind.*
—Ralph Waldo Emerson,
philosopher and writer

❧

*When a deep injury is done to us,
we never recover until we forgive.*
—Alan Paton, *writer*

❧

*Forgiveness is the fragrance the violet
sheds on the heel that has crushed it.*
—Mark Twain, *humorist and writer*

❧

RELEASE OTHERS

Resentment weakens but forgiveness empowers. It takes strength to take the first step toward forgiveness, but that energy will return to you many times over.

The first and the only person to be healed by forgiveness is the person who does the forgiving.
—*Lewis Smedes,* theologian

Here is a mental treatment guaranteed to cure every ill that flesh is heir to: sit for half an hour every night and mentally forgive everyone against whom you have any ill will or antipathy.
—*Charles Fillmore,* founder of the Unity School of Christianity

Forgiveness is crucial to the healing process and it points to an uncynical way of being that has nothing to do with naiveté and everything to do with taking responsibility for our development as human beings.
—*Linus Roache,* actor

If you haven't forgiven someone, it does not hurt that person. They're sleeping at night. You're holding onto that, and all the damage is being done to you internally. So when you learn the power of that—your being angry with that person has no power over them, it only has power over you—you're responsible for it, and you have to make a choice: Do I let this go, or do I hold onto it?

—*Tyler Perry*, playwright and actor, *who overcame depression, homelessness, and abuse*

What's happened in the past has happened, but I'm not mad about it any more. Because when I was angry, it held me back. I can't be held back any more.

—*Mary J. Blige*, singer-songwriter, *who overcame drug and alcohol addiction and child abuse*

I think the act of forgiveness can cut the endless cycle of action and reaction, what Buddhists would call karma. Mostly, I think forgiveness prevents you from reifying things. When you don't forgive another, you objectify that person, hardening him or her into a particular mold. In order to nurse a grudge (wonderful phrase, that, as if you must keep your grudge on life support with round-the-clock care), you always have to think of the other person as "the one who injured me." But that is only a portion of that person's being. So long as you hold on to that frozen image of the other person, the two of you will continue to play out the same dynamic. Forgiveness renders the relationship fluid again, allowing you to see other aspects of that person. And you, too, are freed to exist more fully, not frozen into one posture. Maybe you could say the same about disease—that an unforgiving attitude reifies the disease, forcing it to hold its negative place in your personal cosmology. Then you're trapped in a fixed response, without flexibility of thought and feeling and action.

—*Mark Ian Barasch,* writer, editor, and television producer

All blame is a waste of time. No matter how much fault you find with another, and regardless of how much you blame him, it will not change you. The only thing blame does is to keep the focus off you when you are looking for external reasons to explain your unhappiness or frustration. You may succeed in making another feel guilty about something by blaming him, but you won't succeed in changing whatever it is about you that is making you unhappy.

—**Wayne Dyer,** writer and self-help advocate, who had grown up in foster homes after abandonment by his alcoholic father

In being open to the possibility of understanding and forgiveness, we can perhaps begin to make our first shaky steps towards healing and growth. I think forgiveness is a radical concept: not easy, but potentially miraculous.

—*Annie Lennox,* singer-songwriter

Forgiveness may require confronting others. Healing may come only after you've taken the time to talk things through and clear up misunderstandings.

As the great novelists of manners, the Jane Austens and the Henry Jameses, all knew, the etiquette of communication and miscommunication, the comedy of understanding and misunderstanding, is not only deeply fascinating and entertaining but also profoundly significant. And much more love, more interesting love, is possible than if no difficulties and misunderstandings had occurred in the first place. After all, you can't have the satisfying resolution of the ending if you don't start with conflict and crisis.

—*Michael Davitt Bell,* historian and professor, *on his battle against melanoma*

There are remarkable stories of forgiveness for what many might consider unforgivable acts.

I noticed recently an article that referred to the mothers of the Gugulethu Seven [activists beaten and killed by South African authorities]. I just want to point out that our commission counseled the mothers and told them that a video we had is quite harrowing. But they said they wanted to see it. When we were viewing it, they became so incensed that one of the mothers threw a shoe at one of the police officers who was testifying. Afterwards they said it was horrible, horrible, horrible, but thank you because now we know what happened. . . . One of the mothers, whose son was dragged with a rope, was asked, how do you feel about the police? What would you like to do to this policeman who shot your son? She said, "I don't want anything to happen to him. I don't want him to go to jail. I forgive him."

—*Desmond Tutu,* cleric, activist, and Nobel Peace Prize winner, *on the murder of black activists by the South African government*

I have come to the conclusion that Amy Fisher [who attempted to kill me] has spent enough time in jail as punishment for her crime. It is right and good that I can now say that I forgive Amy Fisher. It is a place I have only been able to reach through grace.

—Mary Jo Buttafuoco, who was shot in the head by Amy Fisher, who was having an affair with Mary Jo's husband, Joey Buttafuoco

A survivor of the Auschwitz concentration camp describes her ultimate act of healing. It happened the day she forgave the Nazi doctors for the torture she suffered in her youth.

I have forgiven the Nazis. I have forgiven everybody. At the fiftieth anniversary observance of the liberation of Auschwitz, in a ceremony attended by my children. . . . I met with a Nazi doctor, Dr. Hans Münch, a former SS doctor at Auschwitz. . . . Dr. Münch treated me with the utmost respect. As we sat down to talk, I said to him, "Here you are—a Nazi doctor from Auschwitz—and here I am—survivor from Auschwitz—and I like you, and that sounds strange to me." We talked about many things . . . And he said, "This is the nightmare I live with." Then, he proceeded to tell me about the operation of the gas chambers and that when the bodies were dead, he had signed the death certificates. . . .

[After I forgave him] I felt a burden of pain was lifted from my shoulders. I was no longer a victim of Auschwitz. I was no longer a prisoner of my tragic past. I was finally free. So I say to everybody:

"FORGIVE YOUR WORST ENEMY. IT WILL HEAL YOUR SOUL AND SET YOU FREE."

The day I forgave the Nazis I forgave my parents because they did not save me from a destiny in Auschwitz and I also forgave myself for hating my parents.

—*Eva Mozes Kor,* Holocaust survivor and Founder and President of Children of Auschwitz—Nazi's Deadly Lab Experiments Survivors (C.A.N.D.L.E.S)

I read this great quote on the train today. It was a Longfellow quote. I'm going to paraphrase it badly, but he said that whenever you see your worst enemy or think of your worst enemy, you need only know his secret sufferings and pains for all animosity to disappear. It's completely true.

—*Zadie Smith,* writer

*Forgiveness
does not equal forgetting.
It is about healing the
memory of the harm,
not erasing it.*

—**Ken Hart**, singer-songwriter

ADDRESS YOUR ANGER

Anger, whether at yourself or at others, is normal. But healing doesn't begin until you flush it out of your system, and that means confronting it in a manner that works for you.

I've come to think over the years that opting to have a temper tantrum is one of the healthiest things I do. Short bursts of rage can be extremely restorative if we live with the constant frustration of chronic pain or extreme stress. We must give vent to these feelings as often as we feel comfortable doing so. It's very hard to value these feelings because we've been taught so consistently that we must never lose control in such an extreme way, but I say if we take certain precautions—that there is never any danger of hurting ourselves or anyone else—let 'er rip!
—***Darlene Cohen***, Zen priest, *on coping with rheumatoid arthritis and other pain*

Feel the pain that's accumulated inside you ever since your childhood. I had to do it to really kill off all the religious myths. In therapy you really feel every painful moment of your life—it's excruciating, you are forced to realise that your pain, the kind that makes you wake up afraid with your heart pounding, is really yours and not the result of somebody up in the sky. It's the result of your parents and your environment.

As I realised this it all started to fall into place. . . . [It's] facing up to reality instead of always looking for some kind of heaven.
—*John Lennon,* singer-songwriter, *on overcoming childhood demons*

On the other hand, realize that your anger will pass as circumstances change.

What ticks me off most about anger is that at the very start of my attempts to read and study Buddhism, when my understanding was at the most elementary level, I was able to quickly grasp how anger was brought on by my own attachments. Whereas I once thought particular people or events could "drive me up a wall," it seemed like only moments after reading my first dharma book that I realized it was me driving myself up the wall, and the wall was a construct of my own making.

Sometime later, I came to understand that the very idea that there is "me" and that there are "others" is at the heart of this illusion—we imagine ourselves separate from other people and too often zealously guard this imagined barrier we have put around ourselves. Our anger is likely the result of our feeling that someone has breached that barrier.

But in Buddhist terms, this is all just a lot of silliness, for we are not separate, there is no "one" to be angry, and the barrier is all an illusion, so how could it be breached?
—*Dinty Moore,* writer and editor

There is no substance to anger. It's an emotion that surfaces and sinks.

Sit in front of a mirror, look at your reflection, and insult it: "You're ugly. You're bad." Then praise it: "You're beautiful. You're good." Regardless of what you say, the image remains simply what it is. Praise and blame are not real in and of themselves. Like an echo, a shadow, a mere reflection, they hold no power to help or harm us.

There is no substance to anger, no thing to find. Once we realize we can't find anger, we can let the mind be. We don't suppress the anger, push it away, or engage it. We simply let the mind rest in the midst of it. We can stay with the energy itself—simply, naturally, remaining aware of it, without attachment, without aversion. Then we find that anger, like desire, isn't really what we thought it was.

—*Chagdud Tulku Rinpoche,* Buddhist teacher

When you meet people who have forgiven, you see their power. You see the strength and courage it takes to forgive in a world dominated by "an eye for an eye." I can suggest that forgiveness is good for you. I can look to people who have forgiven and see how they've healed, and I can teach you to forgive, but it's still your decision and your life.

—*Dr. Fred Luskin,* psychologist and Co-Director of the Stanford–Northern Ireland HOPE Project, an ongoing series of workshops and research projects that investigate the effectiveness of forgiveness methods on the victims of political violence

Forgiveness comes in stages. For many, the first stage is forgiving whomever for whatever happened in your childhood.

I have been reading a wonderful German psychologist called Alice Miller, who says you have to go through a stage of blaming your parents, because if you pretend your childhood was wonderful you will never really find out who you are. Now I accept what happened to me in my childhood. I am no longer angry. It's a great relief that I no longer blame my father, because I have so much more energy for the things I care about.
—***Richard Olivier,*** art consultant and son of actor Laurence Oliver

When you forgive, you create the possibility of a better future—for yourself and for the person you're forgiving.

What I think is you forgive and you forget so you can transform your experiences, not necessarily forget them but transform them, so that they don't haunt you or handicap you or kill you. Rather, you transform them so they can remind you, so that this doesn't happen again. They can prevent this kind of thing from happening to other people. You must do positive things with your experience rather than dwell on the negativity of it. . . . If for example your neighbor killed your family, if you keep seeing them as a perpetual murderer, you will never give them a chance to change; they will never feel at ease around you, and you will never feel at ease either. But when you transform that, when you think, Okay, there was once a time they did that; perhaps they can change. When you do that genuinely, you actually give them a chance to transform. Hence you heal.

—*Ishmael Beah,* former child soldier in Sierra Leone, *on healing after his parents and brothers were murdered and after he himself was forced to "kill too many people to count."*

It's toughest to forgive ourselves. So it's probably best to start with other people. It's almost like peeling an onion. Layer by layer, forgiving others, you really do get to the point where you can forgive yourself.

—*Patty Duke,* actress and survivor of bipolar disorder, drug and alcohol abuse, and sexual abuse in childhood

FORGIVE YOURSELF, TOO

To love yourself, you must forgive yourself of your mistakes—all the things you've done or left undone.

I began trying to figure out what it is to love oneself. Where does love end and narcissism begin? . . . Then I figured that perhaps the start isn't to know whether or not I love myself, but to treat myself in a good way. Love isn't a feeling or a knowing, after all, but action. So I started working on treating myself well, being as nice to myself as I could be.

—*Chaka Khan,* singer-songwriter, *on overcoming drug addiction*

⁓

Quite often if we hold onto the mistake we can't see our own glory in the mirror because we have the mistake between our faces and the mirror, so we can't see what we're capable of being. It is equally important to see the mistake and to forgive oneself for it. You can ask forgiveness of others, but in the end the real forgiveness is in one's own self.

—*Maya Angelou,* poet and Pulitzer prize winner

There are scientific reasons why it's good to have a sense of humor, especially when times are bad. Scientists say the act of laughing relieves muscle tension caused by stress. It boosts endorphins, "natural painkillers," and results in the reduction of cortisol and other hormones that accompany stress and in turn suppress your immune system. Laughing makes you stronger— physically and emotionally. It just might be the most pleasurable way to heal.

LAUGHING

*Humor is just another
defense against the universe.*
—Mel Brooks,
actor, director, and producer

*Sometimes your joy is the source
of your smile, but sometimes your smile
can be the source of your joy.*
—Thich Nhat Hanh, *Buddhist monk*

I'm a birth survivor.
—Bill Maher, *television host*

LET YOURSELF LAUGH

If it relieves stress, allow yourself to laugh. Just because a situation might be serious doesn't mean that *you* must always be serious.

I take Parkinson's disease seriously but I rarely take myself seriously. That's the secret.
—*Michael J. Fox,* actor

Anybody that ever says to you, "Don't laugh at this funeral," or, "Don't try to make that person laugh"—don't listen to them. If that's another road to get you happy for a second, you've given them a second of relief. Believe me, the horror is going to come back and wrap around them again. Don't worry. If you see the widow laughing, let her laugh and say, "Thank you, God, she has one second that she can forget."
—*Joan Rivers,* comedian and talk show host

You can turn painful situations around through laughter. If you can find humor in anything—even poverty—you can survive it.
—*Bill Cosby,* actor, comedian, and TV producer, *whose son was shot to death on a Los Angeles freeway*

*I just think
that laughter is
a real necessity in
healing. . . .*

—**Jennifer Aniston,** actress,
on coping after divorce

Laugh as much as possible. Always laugh; it is the sweetest thing one can do for oneself and one's fellow human being. When people see the laughing face, even if they're jealous of it, their burden is lightened. But do it first for yourself.

—***Maya Angelou,*** poet and Pulitzer prize winner

Humor's essential. . . . Even at the worst, right after [my husband's] second colon cancer, we always found something to laugh about. I would kid him, "While you were in the hospital, I did purchase a black dress, just in case." We just made jokes. And we still do. It's what gets you through.

—***Meredith Vieira,*** journalist and talk show host, *on coping with her husband having multiple sclerosis and colon cancer*

I think laughter is the best thing for everything. You know what I mean? Loosens up the muscles. . . . I think it is all about fooling your body into thinking you feel well.

—***Jonathan Ames,*** writer, *on conquering depression*

Humor can also be a natural way to tap into deeper truths.

My brand of humor, that so-called dark, self-deprecating humor, can be painful. Painfully honest. But it's the kind of humor we grow from—that ability to laugh at ourselves; to make fun of our human foibles. If my humor has a subtext it's, "Don't take yourself so seriously. Lighten up."
—*Julie Ann Peters,* writer

⚜

Perhaps I know best why it is man alone who laughs; he alone suffers so deeply that he had to invent laughter.
—*Friedrich Nietzsche,* philosopher

⚜

Being happy is the most important thing to me, because we weren't put here to be miserable. We were put here to do the best we can, and we should take our energy and improve our state of being. I think people have had enough negativity. The reason dance music is so popular is because people want to party. They want to celebrate. I'm tired of hearing guys sing about how shitty life is.
—*Lenny Kravitz,* singer-songwriter

To love is to suffer. To avoid suffering, one must not love. But then, one suffers from not loving. Therefore, to love is to suffer; not to love is to suffer; to suffer is to suffer. To be happy is to love. To be happy, then, is to suffer, but suffering makes one unhappy. Therefore, to be happy, one must love or love to suffer or suffer from too much happiness.

—**Woody Allen,** actor, playwright, and writer

I believe so strongly in the importance of humor. . . . There are so many tension-producing realities in our society, and certainly these cannot be ignored, but humor gives us a crucial, compensating balance and it should not be trivialized. I believe in the healing powers of humor, in its ability to lubricate our passage through the ongoing frustrations and difficulties that life contrives . . .

—*Stephen Kellogg,* children's book author and illustrator

The hardest thing you can do is smile when you are ill, in pain, or depressed. But this no-cost remedy is a necessary first half-step if you are to start on the road to recovery.

—*Allen Klein,* record label executive

BELIEVE HUMOR IS MEDICINE

Many people swear that maintaining a sense of humor through their setbacks helped more than taking medication.

A good, real, unrestrained, hearty laugh is a sort of glorified internal massage, performed rapidly and automatically. It manipulates and revitalizes corners and unexplored crannies of the system that are unresponsive to most other exercise methods.

—*Anonymous*

Mirth is God's medicine. Everybody ought to bathe in it.

—**Henry Ward Beecher,** clergyman

My father was an alcoholic, and my mother had to raise three children essentially on her own. So I sort of became the adult and had to deal with the death of my father and help my mother cope. I'm sure that having a sense of humor helped.

—**Nathan Lane,** actor, *on coping with his father's alcoholism*

Once [after my stroke] I told my wife that I thought I wanted breakfast in bed the next morning, she said the old joke, "If you want breakfast in bed, sleep in the kitchen." That's a good laugh. But, she knows that I need a kick in the ass. She's so funny. My wife says that she thinks I have to give more speeches since my stroke than before my stroke. Then I'd say, "Oh God, I have to give this speech and I don't think I'm going to be able to talk." And she says, "Well, do you have anything to say?" She makes me laugh. A sense of humor is so important. If you can laugh at yourself and laugh at others . . . it's very important.

—*Kirk Douglas*, actor and film producer, *on recovering from a stroke*

I decided a positive attitude and strong faith were going to have to be my illness-conquering tools. . . . I decided the least I could do was to start smiling and at a time when that was the LAST thing I felt like doing. When they sent me down the hall for an EEG (electroencephalogram), it was a turning point in my hospital stay. All those wires glued to someone's head would in many patients induce fear, anxiety or at least a visual flashback of Boris Karloff playing Frankenstein. When they wheeled me back to my bed, I flipped over the bed stand placemat, retrieved a pen and drew my first cartoon. When I presented it to the lab technicians they laughed out loud and taped it up on the wall. It was all the incentive

I needed. Pretty soon everything became a cartoon . . . the medical tests, other patients, and the English language itself. I was provided a stack of white paper and a black marking pen. I soon discovered this self-prescribed cartoon medicine was a wonderful tool for healing and recovery . . . and it changed my life.

—*Jo Lee Dibert-Fitko,* cartoonist, *on healing from a brain tumor and spiral meningitis*

Humor is a crack in your problems. It relieves the pressure, which might be enough for you to begin to see your situation in a different way.

Laughter gives us distance. It allows us to step back from an event, deal with it and then move on.

—*Bob Newhart,* comedian and actor

Humor is a healing balm and one of the highest expressions of the human spirit. I was at a gathering where the speaker was saying, "There are probably people here who have not been able to achieve a goal that they've set for themselves, and maybe they blame a boss or a spouse. How many blame a boss? How many blame a spouse? Anything else?" There's this long pause, and I say, "The Supreme Court!" It slightly derailed the discussion. There've been times when I did take myself deadly seriously. But those times are long past.

—**Al Gore,** politician, businessman, and environmentalist, *on healing after the 2000 U.S. presidential election in which he won the popular vote but lost the presidency in court*

A person without a sense of humor is like a wagon without springs. It's jolted by every pebble on the road.

—*Henry Ward Beecher,* clergyman and activist

Somewhere between 90 and 99 percent of experiments will fail. And in order to cope with that, you need a sense of humor. You need to understand that, yeah, it didn't work, but there's got to be something good that came out of it. You must have learned something, or there's got to be something funny about how it didn't work, or something that we can be happy about that will stimulate us to try it again the next day.

—*Bert Vogelstein,* cancer researcher, *on handling failure in the laboratory*

*At the height of laughter,
the universe is
flung into a kaleidoscope
of new possibilities.*

—**Jean Houston**, spiritual guide

Victims of war have attributed humor as the quality that helped them endure and heal from wartime atrocities.

When I was interviewed for Spielberg and they asked me what I thought was the reason I survived [in the Nazi concentration camps], they probably expected me to answer good fortune or other things. I said that I thought it was laughter and humor . . . I only thought how not to take things seriously. Because it was absurd all that time, it was unconceivable, that they could do those things to people.
—**from interviews of Holocaust survivors by *Chaya Ostrower*,** psychologist

Laughter sets the spirit free to move through even the most tragic of circumstances. It helps us shake our heads clear, get our feet back under us, restoring our sense of balance and purpose. Humor is integral to our peace of mind and to our ability to go beyond survival.
—***Gerald Coffee*,** U.S. army captain, *on surviving as a POW in Vietnam for seven years*

Everyone heals in their own time

and in their own way, but many swear that it helps

to live your normal, active life even through times

of hardship. Don't ignore your problems, but don't

dwell on them either. If you can, force yourself to

do the things you would normally do—go to work,

honor your commitments, see your friends. Heal

by living in the moment.

LIVING

*This is as true in everyday life as
it is in battle: we are given one life and the
decision is ours whether to wait for
circumstances to make up our mind,
or whether to act, and in acting, to live.*
—Omar Bradley, *general*

*You must understand,
I don't have to be happy to be happy.*
—Juliette Binoche, *actress*

*Life is full of misery,
loneliness, and suffering—and it's
all over much too soon.*
—Woody Allen,
director, writer, and comedian

BE ACTIVE

Everyday activities—exercising, running errands, doing your job—may be surprisingly therapeutic. As hard as it may seem, try to find meaning and purpose in all the usual activities that give your life normalcy and structure.

For me, being out on the road, when you've got something to do every day, is good therapy.
—*Willie Nelson,* singer-songwriter

I think the best coping strategies are the healthy coping strategies that have worked for us before, so exercising, talking to people we're close to, working. I think working is actually very healthy for most people to have someplace to go and to feel productive and just distract ourselves from our own thoughts.
—*Barbara Rothbaum,* psychologist

Just because you're going through a tough time doesn't mean you should absolve yourself of your responsibilities.

This rich guy lives in this town, and he goes to work every day in this big factory that he owns, and he goes by this very crippled old beggar in the street. And he always gives him a couple of shekels every day. This goes on for years. Well, the business starts doing poorly, and the rich guy is not so rich and he goes to work that day and he may or may not be able to keep the company open and doesn't give the guy any shekels. And the guy says, "Excuse me, where are my shekels?" And the [rich] guy says, "Well, I'm not doing well." And the beggar says, "Well, what does that have to do with me?"

Now at first you go, "A beggar being so self-centered?" But Jewish stories are very deep. . . . What it says is, no matter what you're going through, you owe others . . . no matter what you're going through, pick up a phone and call somebody at home sick, or go down to the shelter and help somebody learn to read, [and] you are ennobled and your depression is lifted.
—*Laura Schlesinger,* cultural commentator and radio host

[T]hey say if you want to get all the air out of a glass, what do you do? There's no way to do it but fill it with something else. And that something else is joy of living, reading, being creative, know you're doing the right thing. And that got me to thinking.

—**Mary Tyler Moore,** on recovering from alcohol addiction

Work, especially the type of work that forces you to perform and be among others, may actually be a reprieve.

All of us who are actors in the theater look on it as Doctor Theater, you know. You get down there. You're with your colleagues. The energy starts to come back. And by the time you've got your makeup and your hair, your wig on and your costume, you walk out there. And for a period of time, you no longer have cancer.

—**Lynn Redgrave,** actor, *on coping with breast cancer*

The morning that I picked [my son's] coffin out, I [hosted] ten—or five "Scrabbles" that day and did five the next day. And it was really odd—well, I would go on television and do a game, and . . . would act like nothing was going on; it was just normal, like in normal time, normal sequence. And then, just the minute [we] were finished with it, I'd walk in and cry for 15 minutes.

—**Chuck Woolery,** game show host, *on coping after the death of his son in a motorcycle accident*

Force yourself to be part of the world, even when you don't want any part of it.

You can become addicted to that pain. I used to close my door and I kind of enjoyed it in a way. I know now I have a choice to get out of it or to stay in it. Now I don't enjoy it. Now I tell myself, Don't ask why is it happening, but what are you going to do to get out of it. The way to get out of it is just to carry on and say, "Listen, let's go ahead and get out of that room."

—**Sir Elton John,** *singer-songwriter, on recovering from depression and substance abuse*

When you're depressed, it makes a lot of difference how you stand. The worst thing you can do is straighten up and hold your head high because then you'll start to feel better.

—**Charles Schulz,** cartoonist and illustrator, *said by the character Charlie Brown*

I did have a miscarriage and I'm still coping with that. I could have said, "I'm not doing any press for this film. See ya later. I'm not coming out until I am completely healed." But I don't know if that will ever happen. It's been awful, but I will move forward day by day. I'm dealing with this, and I find I'm stronger than I thought. Although there are times when I don't feel that strong. I mean, there are times when I feel really, really weak. I think it is just that when you are a mother, and you have two people who are dependent on you, and look to you to be guided, you have to rise to that occasion.

—*Nicole Kidman,* actress, *on recovering from a miscarriage*

The busy bee has no time for sorrow.
—*William Blake,* writer

You never saw a very busy person who was unhappy.
—*Dorothy Dix,* journalist

TAKE CARE OF YOUR BODY

Your mind is connected to your body and vice versa; your emotional and physical health are inseparable. To heal the mind, take care of your body. Listen to it.

Sleep is that golden chain that ties health and our bodies together.
—*Thomas Dekker,* actor

❧

Begin to see yourself as a soul with a body rather than a body with a soul.
—*Wayne Dyer,* self-help advocate

❧

To keep the body in good health is a duty . . . otherwise we shall not be able to keep our mind strong and clear.
—*Buddha*

❧

I have a holistic attitude to health—it has to be a combination of physical, spiritual and emotional care. It's about listening to your body. Sometimes I need to run, other times to meditate, sometimes I need to dance with my kids, and sometimes I just need a good meal. I don't have a regime.

—*Elle Macpherson,* model

It sounds so corny, but our bodies are our vessels. We have to get through our entire lives in this body. We're taught that we don't have a choice about our bodies, when actually we're responsible for them. Your body doesn't take care of you. You take care of it.

—*Cameron Diaz,* actress

I finally realized that being grateful to my body was key to giving more love to myself.

—*Oprah Winfrey,* talk show host

Keeping your body healthy is an expression of gratitude to the whole cosmos—the trees, the clouds, everything.

—*Thich Nhat Hanh,* Buddhist monk

Just as your mind influences your body, so does your body influence your mind. If you're aware of your body, you may be able to goad yourself into being in a healthier emotional state.

. . . I was walking a little too hard, and I thought, "Walk slower, feel your ass going from left to right. Get that sway back." No matter what the circumstances, you can change how you feel by noticing what your body is doing and taking it easier. And miraculously, though not always, that can have a positive effect on the circumstances, too.

—*Liz Phair,* singer-songwriter

My times of being erotic, sensual, sexual, and loving with a lover are the most blissful, beautiful, spiritual, healing moments I experience in my life.

—*Annie Sprinkle,* performance artist

Nothing lifts me out of a bad mood better than a hard workout on my treadmill. It never fails. Exercise is nothing short of a miracle.

—*Cher,* singer-songwriter and actress

Exercise ferments the humors, casts them into their proper channels, throws off redundancies, and helps nature in those secret distributions, without which the body cannot subsist in its vigor, nor the soul act with cheerfulness.
—*Joseph Addison*, politician and writer

The best six doctors anywhere

And no one can deny it

Are sunshine, water, rest, and air

Exercise and diet.

These six will gladly you attend

If only you are willing

Your mind they'll ease

Your will they'll mend

And charge you not a shilling.

—Nursery rhyme

LIVE IN THE PRESENT

Living means living in the present—not in the past or in the future. Living in the moment diminishes anxiety about the future and pain associated with the past. Focus on valuing what you have *now*.

Forget about tomorrow, because at this very second, is there anything you need, or is there anything wrong? And you'll find yourself going, "No." It takes a conscious effort from me, because I can start worrying.

—*Sandra Bullock,* actress

What's the point of loving my mother since she is only going to die and what's the point of loving myself since I am only going to die and what's the point of loving this book since it is only going to go out in the maelstrom of publication? . . . I have remembered only my paltry ego and its bruises. I am thinking of endings, not process. Whenever I think of endings, I get stuck.

—*Erica Jong,* writer, *on coping with her mother's terminal illness*

I have never savored life with such gusto as I do now. I have never appreciated a quiet moment with a friend as much, a quiet moment with a book and I think part of that is my obsession with being older and time going faster and it's become increasingly sweeter for me. I've never felt more comfortable in my skin, I've never enjoyed life as much and I feel so lucky.

—*Candice Bergen,* actress, *on accepting her mortality*

Life is really short. Even if you live to be 90 years old, it goes by in the wink of an eye. You don't have anything to say over when you're going to die. The only choice you really have is to try to live it up while you're here, and don't postpone happiness.

—*Bruce Willis,* actor, *on the death of his brother from pancreatic cancer*

If you observe a really happy man, you will find him building a boat, writing a symphony, educating his child, growing double dahlias or looking for dinosaur eggs in the Gobi Desert. He will not be searching for happiness as if it were a collar button that had rolled under the radiator, striving for it as a goal in itself. He will have become aware that he is happy in the course of living life twenty-four crowded hours of each day.

—**W. Beran Wolfe,** psychiatrist

I believe the best therapy one can indulge in is to play hard, because life is blowing by at such an alarming rate that if we stay serious about it, by the time we want to play we're going to be ready for the undertaker.
—*Sylvester Stallone,* actor

᧑

Finish each day and be done with it. You have done what you could; some blunders and absurdities have crept in; forget them as soon as you can. Tomorrow is a new day; you shall begin it serenely and with too high a spirit to be encumbered with your old nonsense.
—*Ralph Waldo Emerson,* philosopher and writer

᧑

The aims of life are the best defense against death.
—*Primo Levi,* writer, chemist, and Holocaust survivor

MEDITATE

Many people find meditation a way to "be in the moment." By repeating a mantra or focusing on and following their breath, they find they can peacefully coexist with their problems. Meditation produces a soothing sense of awareness.

Meditation is a very important aspect of all the approaches that one can use in quantum healing, because it allows you to experience your own source. When you experience your own source, you realize that you are not the patterns and eddies of desire and memory that flow and swirl in your consciousness. . . . You are the thinker behind the thought, the observer behind the observation, the flow of attention, the flow of awareness, the unbounded ocean of consciousness. When you have that on the experiential level, you spontaneously realize that you have choices, and that you can exercise these choices, not through some sheer will power but spontaneously.

—*Deepak Chopra,* medical doctor and writer

If I had not already been meditating, I would certainly have had to start. I've treated my own depression for many years with exercise and meditation, and I've found that to be a tremendous help.

—**Judy Collins**, singer-songwriter, *on surviving depression and the suicide of her son*

Anywhere I am, twice a day I go off and meditate. Twenty minutes in the morning, twenty minutes in the evening is the deal. And things start getting better. That's the reason you do it. All the stresses and fears and anxieties begin to recede and a really beautiful inner kind of energy and happiness grows, and you enjoy the doing of things so much more, and those things that used to knock you out don't have the same power any more. Things get smoother and way more fun.

—**David Lynch**, filmmaker

Give yourself some mental space whenever you need it. If possible, give yourself some physical refuge as well.

You must have a room, or a certain hour or so a day, where you don't know what was in the newspaper that morning . . . a place where you can simply experience and bring forth what you are and what you might be.
—*Joseph Campbell,* writer and orator

I do like people, but I'm a loner and need downtime. If I don't go in and recharge, my fuse is short. And it depends on the quality of the break. You can rest a lot in an hour or have a whole day and not do it properly. One way I get a quality recharge is to connect with nature. To experience something that's bigger than me.
—*Lili Taylor,* actress

I go to nature to be soothed and healed, and to have my senses put in order.
—*John Burroughs,* naturalist and writer

To sit in the shade on a fine day, and look upon verdure is the most perfect refreshment.
—*Jane Austen,* writer

You need moments of repose to open yourself up to any kind of enlightenment. If you just wake up, grab your breakfast and run the rest of the day, and dance yourself silly until you collapse, you're probably not giving yourself any moment to let anything else in.

—**Sir Mick Jagger,** singer-songwriter

Healing requires persistence. To heal, you need to continue when you want to quit; be optimistic when you feel pessimistic; examine yourself when you want to escape yourself; and adapt even when you don't want to change. Persistence is not only a survival mechanism. It is what gives life meaning and purpose.

PERSISTING

If you are going through hell, keep going.
—Sir Winston Churchill, *prime minister of the UK and Nobel Laureate in Literature*

Although the world is full of suffering, it is also full of the overcoming of it.
—Helen Keller, *deaf and blind author and activist*

In three words I can sum up everything I've learned about life: It goes on.
—Robert Frost, *poet*

When my syndicated show got canceled, the next day I still knew how to write jokes. That was a huge revelation.
—Jon Stewart, *comedian, producer, and TV host*

NEVER GIVE UP

Every survivor has a story of how grateful they are that they never gave up, even when they came close to doing so.

I know it sounds cliché, but you have to find a way to hold on because time really does heal all wounds.

—*Halle Berry,* actress, *on recovering after her divorce*

Never give up. Get the best help you can. Keep trying, keep loving, keep giving, keep looking for the right answers, and love, love, love, love. Don't listen to the words, just listen to your heart.

—*Danielle Steel,* writer, *advice on coping with a person who is mentally ill, after her son committed suicide at age 19 after a lifelong battle with bipolar disorder*

Funny how losing my hair made me worry less about a bad haircut and how losing a breast made me feel so confident in other ways . . . the things I used to be critical about my looks really seemed less important. I could not believe what was still there when everyone else left. What was left was bold and powerful and hanging on with claws screaming, "My show must go on! . . . Don't give up now!"

—**Geralyn Lucas**, journalist and television producer, *on recovering from breast cancer*

Most of the important things in the world have been accomplished by people who have kept on trying when there seemed to be no hope at all.

—*Dale Carnegie,* self-help advocate and writer

There is a story in the Bible of a woman that had a disease, and when she heard that Jesus was coming into her town, sought to be there. And the Bible says she struggled through that crowd so she could simply touch him. And when she did, she was healed. But imagine had she said, OK, there's a crowd here, it's too big, I can't really get there, and would have given up, then she would not have been healed. So I tell people all the time to never give up.

—*Larry King,* TV talk show host and survivor of a massive heart attack

I'm very up, I'm confident. I've been in a number of fights in my life, and this is just another one, and I'm sure we will be able to prevail.

—*John McCain,* senator, *on recovering from cancer surgery*

It was almost like, how could I [give up] when all these people, you know, in addition to my family were behind me and believing in me. And I thought, no, I can't give up and I'm not going to give up.

—**Trisha Meili**, Central Park jogger raped and beaten comatose

Pain is temporary. It may last a minute, or an hour, or a day, or a year, but eventually it will subside and something else will take its place. If I quit, however, it lasts forever.

—**Lance Armstrong,** cyclist and seven-time winner of the Tour de France, *on overcoming testicular cancer*

WEAKEN YOUR FEARS

People who have overcome major problems have found that the only way to weaken their fears is to face them. Confront your fears however you can.

You gain strength, courage, and confidence by each experience in which you really stop to look fear in the face. You are able to say to yourself, "I have lived through this horror. I can take the next thing that comes along."
—*Eleanor Roosevelt,* political leader and First Lady (1933–1945)

I went out to Coney Island one night and went on every single thing that terrified me. The parachute jump, roller coasters—everything that scared me—over and over again.
—*Edward Albee,* playwright, *on overcoming his fears*

How to defeat terrorism? Don't be terrorized. Don't let fear rule your life. Even if you are scared.
—*Salman Rushdie,* writer, *on coping after the September 11, 2001, terrorist attacks*

I must not fear. Fear is the mind-killer. Fear is the little-death that brings total obliteration. I will face my fear. I will permit it to pass over me and through me. And when it has gone past I will turn the inner eye to see its path. When the fear has gone there will be nothing. Only I will remain.

—**Frank Herbert,** writer, *from the* Dune *series*

[When I was diagnosed with cancer] I cried like everyone does. But something came over me. I rolled up my sleeves and told my doctors, 'I will be the best patient you ever had.' I approached cancer like a competition—stand up straight, tell me what to do and I'll win. Being able to focus under pressure—I've used that so many times in my life.

—**Peggy Fleming**, figure skater and Olympic gold medalist, *on surviving breast cancer*

TAKE CONTROL OF THE PROCESS

Take charge of your own healing. Be part of the solution—not a passive victim.

There are two big forces at work, external and internal. We have very little control over external forces such as tornadoes, earthquakes, floods, disasters, illness and pain. What really matters is the internal force. How do I respond to those disasters? Over that I have complete control.

—*Leo Buscaglia,* teacher

The difference for me is between being victimized, terrorized, numbed by reading about different disasters, or reducing the anxiety by getting up and doing something about it, at whatever level. Get up, do something—whatever it is. If you actively do something, it will stop making you feel like a victim and you'll start feeling like part of the solution, which is just a huge benefit to your body and your psyche.

—*Ted Danson,* actor, *on coping with fear of terrorism and other disasters*

Never allow yourself to be made a victim. Accept no one's definition of your life, but define yourself.

—**Harvey S. Firestone,** industrialist

When Andy Grove was diagnosed with prostate cancer, he took it upon himself to explore all his options for treatment, which gave him a better sense of control over the situation.

The whole thing reminds me of the uncomfortable feeling I experienced when I first sought out investment advice. After a while, it dawned on me that financial advisers, well intentioned and competent as they might have been, were all favoring their own financial instruments. . . . Similarly, given the structure of the medical practice associated with prostate cancer, that's the only viable choice any patient has. If you look after your investments, I think you should look after your life as well. Investigate things, come to your own conclusions, don't take any one recommendation as gospel.

—*Andrew Grove,* cofounder and chairman of Intel (1997–2005), *on overcoming prostate cancer*

If depression is creeping up and must be faced, learn something about the nature of the beast: You may escape without a mauling.

—*R. W. Shepherd,* psychologist

There are many ways you can make yourself feel as if you have more control over your situation. And once you *feel* as if you have more control, you actually do have more control.

[When I got cancer] I visualized [my immune system] as a *Star Wars*–like machine. It was shooting laser beams like death rays at these very clumsy, stupid [breast cancer] cells that didn't know the time of day, destroying them, and the white cells were rushing in to take them off to the dump heap.

—*Rue McClanahan, actress, on overcoming breast cancer*

A healing totem helped writer Anne Lamott when she and her boyfriend broke up.

[My friend and I] were walking into town one day, I was very depressed, and I just put a quarter in a gumball machine because I was bored. This stupid little turquoise rubber shoe came out. And I just loved it. I could wrap my fingers around it. It tethered me to the earth or something . . . Pat, whom I was staying with, would make fun of me, but I couldn't put it down.

When her situation changed in life and things got hard for her, one morning I left the blue shoe for her to have with a little note that said I would walk her through these challenges; she didn't have to worry, but I thought she needed the blue shoe. And she couldn't put it down. It was so nutty. She was very fancy and much older than I was, and yet the same thing happened for her: Once she held it, she couldn't put it down. Six months later things changed in my life and she gave it back to me. We did this back-and-forth for years.

—*Anne Lamott,* writer, *on recovering from a breakup*

The most important part is feeling that you have enough control over the situation. This will give you the momentum to move on with your life.

When something goes wrong, if you can find any little bit you could be responsible for, it automatically flips it around to where you are in control again. Something bad happens to me, and I go, "I don't like that this happened, but how can I fix it so it doesn't happen again?" It doesn't mean I don't suffer sometimes. But you can turn things around.

—*John Travolta,* actor

∾

Control your destiny or somebody else will.
—*Jack Welch*, former chairman and CEO of General Electric (1981–2001)

How do geese know when to fly to the sun? Who tells them the seasons? How do we, humans know when it is time to move on? As with the migrant birds, so surely with us, there is a voice within if only we would listen to it, that tells us certainly when to go forth into the unknown.
—*Elisabeth Kubler-Ross*, psychiatrist

BE PATIENT

Healing is a slow process. It takes patience.

My recovery from manic depression has been an evolution, not a sudden miracle.
—*Patty Duke*, actress and survivor of bipolar disorder, drug and alcohol abuse, and sexual abuse in childhood

The first year was hard for me to deal with. The second year was a little bit easier, but still difficult. It took me five years to get it out of me. It was a difficult moment, a difficult time.

—**Earvin "Magic" Johnson,** basketball player, *on coping with his HIV diagnosis*

Arm yourself with a battery of slogans, build new daily habits, meet new people, take up new interests, and perhaps find the right antidepressant medication and/or the right therapist or guide. . . . We heal. Sometimes it takes a few weeks. More normally it takes months. Often it takes more than two years of separation. But some glorious morning you will notice you haven't thought of your hurtful partner in a week or more. Your enemy is no longer in your head.

—**Helen Fisher,** anthropologist, *on healing from heartache after a romantic breakup*

While grief is fresh, every attempt to divert only irritates. You must wait till it be digested, and then amusement will dissipate the remains of it.

—**Samuel Johnson,** poet and essayist

When people start out, all they ask for is 24 hours to, you know, stay away from that drink or that drug. And then you put one 24 hours together with another one and another one, and eventually you get kind of proud of it.

—**Betty Ford,** former First Lady (1974–1977) and founder of the Betty Ford Center for Substance Abuse and Addiction, *on overcoming her alcohol addiction*

Grief is as palpable as pneumonia, as a disease. It has a beginning, a middle and an end. To each individual it changes. But that grief—you can be led through grief, out of grief. You heal like it's a wound. It's a terrible, terrible pain. But the pain eventually subsides.

—**William Shatner**, actor, on the accidental death of his wife by drowning

In fact, healing, in one form or another, may be a lifelong process. Consider it part of being alive.

Happiness is the process, not the place. . . . Many of us think that when we get everything just right, and obtain certain goals and circumstances, everything will be in place and we will be happy. . . . But once we get everything in place, we still need new goals and activities. The Princess could not just stop when she got the Prince.

—*Ed Diener,* psychologist

My recovery from addiction began when I stopped using alcohol and other drugs, but the only solution to my disease is to stay stopped. And, as you know too well, anyone can quit— it's not starting again that's the hard part. For while researchers and scientists tell us that our disease originates somewhere in the brain, it also lingers in the deepest regions of the human soul. . . . We have a disease that cannot be cured, and recovery requires that we work hard every day to be humble, honest, tolerant, forgiving, and, always, teachable.

—*William Cope Moyers,* journalist, *on recovering from drug and alcohol addiction and skin cancer*

Remember: Healing happens step by step (sometimes literally).

One Monday morning, the doctors came in and said to me, "On Friday we are going to ask you to take three steps." That was the first time I ever remember visualizing. Looking back now, I didn't realize it then. I worked all week, lying on my bed, thinking what it would be like and how I would somehow manage to take three steps. Friday morning came and somehow I did manage. And that was really the start of my recovery.

—*Tenley Albright,* figure skater and Olympic gold medalist, *on recovering from polio*

What saves a man is to take a step. Then another step.

—*Antoine de Saint Exupéry,* writer and pilot

How poor are they who have not patience! What wound did ever heal but by degrees.

—*William Shakespeare,* writer

What does it take to remove your-

self from anxiety, pain, and despair? Transcending

is seeing your situation in a broader, philosophical

light. Try to place your own life in the context of all

life on earth. Attempt to free yourself from the lim-

itations of your condition. Remember you are part

of this ceaseless cycle of life; your pain is part of all

pain, and your healing is part of all healing.

TRANSCENDING

꧂

*To the degree that you are
attached is the degree that you will suffer.*
—Anonymous

꧂

*At such moments, you realize
that you and the other are, in fact, one.
It's a big realization. Survival is the second
law of life. The first is that we are all one.*
—Joseph Campbell, *professor and orator*

꧂

*When you can't remember why
you're hurt, that's when you're healed.*
—Jane Fonda, *actress*

꧂

STEP OUTSIDE YOURSELF

With healing comes wisdom. Many people who have rebounded from a major setback—the loss of a loved one, a major disease, a striking disappointment—have an expanded worldview. They have developed a new philosophy of life.

My accident really brought all those flashcards of clarity and truth together that have happened throughout my life.

—*Rick Allen,* drummer, *on recovering from a car accident in which he lost his arm*

If you are distressed by anything external, the pain is not due to the thing itself but to your own estimate of it; and this you have the power to revoke at any moment.

—*Marcus Aurelius,* Roman emperor

Think of it this way: Our bodies and brains are only part of a greater reality of which we know very little.

I am regarded as "Nick, the weirdo," because what I do is I have a dark field microscope in my bedroom and I'm constantly looking at blood, whether it's my blood or my son's blood. And I put it upon a high-definition screen. . . . Because the longer you spend looking at your blood—first of all, it's another universe. It's absolutely another universe. It's vibrant. Cells vibrate, and it's alive, and you see fibrogen and you see—you see bacteria. You see white cells moving and surrounding things. And the longer you watch your blood, the less this means anything, because this is really the thinnest veneer of facade.

—*Nick Nolte*, actor and producer

Some see several selves—a physical self and a spiritual self—and imagine their spiritual self separating from their body.

I started working the physical very hard in a meditational way by walking for hours and hours. I found that, eventually, the higher self, the spiritual self, starts to float away from you. There's this moment when you're like a child with a balloon—the child is the physical part of you, and the balloon is your soul, finally getting an overview of what life is.

—*Julian Cope*, musician

Personal transformation can and does have global effects. As we go, so goes the world, for the world is us. The revolution that will save the world is ultimately a personal one.

—Marianne Williamson, lecturer and spiritual leader

Those who have had a near-death experience claim that it has given them a new handle on life.

I get to be not afraid of dying and I get to tell other people that it is a fabulous thing and that death is a gift. And not that you should kill yourself, but that when death comes to you, as it will, that it is a glorious and beautiful thing. This kind of giant vortex of white light was upon me and I kind of—poof—sort of took off into this glorious, bright, bright, bright white light and I started to see and be met by some of my friends.

—*Sharon Stone, actress, on recovering from a near-death experience*

          ❧

I was able to look over the edge. I got a little glimpse of what was the next step. I didn't see a light some people see, but I had a wonderful feeling of bliss and warmth. The bottom line is "love." That sounds corny, but it was just lovely, uplifting.

—*Larry Hagman, actor, on a near-death experience during a liver transplant*

EXAMINE YOUR MIND

Observe the distracting thoughts that pop into your head. Realize that sad, anxious, and painful thoughts are impermanent. Try to train your mind to overcome them by detaching yourself from them.

You sit for long periods of time, and during the intensive weeks, which are one out of every month, you sit for about eighteen hours a day. You begin to examine the panic of your mind. So it seems to be that if you can stay still for any amount of time, anything more than a minute or two, which we rarely ever do, some things are disclosed to you. Of course, you shake your legs after meals and go to the bathroom, that sort of thing, but basically there's nothing but stillness for about eighteen hours a day, and everything comes up.

—*Leonard Cohen,* singer-songwriter and poet

Spiritual awareness is the only way that healing can occur. If I may take the risk of defining what a spiritual experience is, it is one in which pure awareness reveals itself to you as the maker of reality—where you suddenly discover through insight or meditation or a freak accident that your essential nature is spiritual, non-material. . . . With that ability comes a major insight: I am the thinker and not the thought. That insight, at a deep level of awareness, is enough to cause a change in one's consciousness, and a spontaneous change in one's biology.

—**Deepak Chopra,** medical doctor and writer

The source of anxiety lies in the future. If you can keep the future out of mind, you can forget your worries.

—**Milan Kundera,** writer and playwright

Or detach yourself from these thoughts by creating beautiful places in your own mind where you can take refuge.

The mind I love must have wild places, a tangled orchard where dark damsons drop in the heavy grass, an overgrown little wood, the chance of a snake or two, a pool that nobody's fathomed the depth of, and paths threaded with flowers planted by the mind.

—**Katherine Mansfield,** writer

SEE YOURSELF AS PART OF
A GREATER WHOLE

It may be surprisingly liberating (and healing) to release your ego and acknowledge that you are part of all life. Your life may be impermanent, but your influence extends beyond your physical self.

A human being is part of a whole, called by us the "Universe," a part limited in time and space. He experiences himself, his thoughts and feelings as something separated from the rest—a kind of optical delusion of his consciousness. This delusion is a kind of prison for us, restricting us to our personal desires and to affection for a few persons nearest us. Our task must be to free ourselves from this prison by widening our circles of compassion to embrace all living creatures and the whole of nature in its beauty.

—**Albert Einstein**, physicist

Those who have learned by experience what physical pain and bodily anguish mean, belong together all the world over; they are united by a secret bond. One and all they know the horrors of suffering to which man can be exposed, and one and all they know the longing to be free from pain.

—**Albert Schweitzer,** theologian and Nobel Peace prize winner

Some find it helpful to perceive themselves as energy or patterns of energy. When they're sick or depressed, they've lost their energy. When they're healed, they say their energy is back, that they feel whole again.

You are energy. You are not in your physical body—your physical body is in you. Most disease, whether it is a physical illness or a chronic life pattern, is associated with blocks and disruptions in this flow of energy. When a healer opens a person's energy and creates more flow, it can affect a person physically, emotionally, mentally and/or spiritually. A person may, after a healing, have more awareness of emotional patterns relating to a physical problem after a healing. A person may also experience more rapid healing of a wound or illness. A spiritual shift might involve feeling peace, love, and connection to one's true essence.

—*Barbara Brennan,* physicist and spiritual healer

༄

What is soul? It's like electricity—we don't really know what it is, but it's a force that can light a room.

—*Ray Charles,* singer-songwriter

Others use the analogy of water. See yourself as a drop of water or a stream.

Empty your mind, be formless, shapeless—like water. Now you put water into a cup, it becomes the cup, you put water into a bottle, it becomes the bottle, you put it in a teapot, it becomes the teapot. Now water can flow or it can crash. Be water, my friend.

—*Bruce Lee,* actor

⨎

Water is fluid, soft, and yielding. But water will wear away rock, which is rigid and cannot yield. As a rule, whatever is fluid, soft, and yielding will overcome whatever is rigid and hard. This is another paradox: what is soft is strong.

—*Lao-Tzu,* philosopher

Or a landmass:

No man is an island, entire of itself; every man is a piece of the continent, a part of the main; if a clod be washed away by the sea.

—*John Donne,* poet

I am a frayed and nibbled survivor in a fallen world, and I am getting along. I am aging and eaten and have done my share of eating too. I am not washed and beautiful, in control of a shining world in which everything fits, but instead am wondering awed about on a splintered wreck I've come to care for, whose gnawed trees breathe a delicate air, whose bloodied and scarred creatures are my dearest companions, and whose beauty bats and shines not in its imperfections but overwhelmingly in spite of them . . .

—**Annie Dillard**, writer

EMBRACE MORTALITY

Enjoy the time you have in this life. Accept that all things have beginnings and endings. Life is measured in more ways than the number of heartbeats.

My brother. I still can't believe I won't see him again. I can't even talk about it. But death is a comfort because that's what saves you. Suffering, cancer, some horrible disease, I'm terrified of pain. Death will just take you away from that. So what's to be afraid of? It's a cessation of pain. What more could you ask? It's like the good nurse.

—**Maurice Sendak,** children's writer, *on recovering from the death of his brother*

In the beginning, I was afraid of dying from AIDS, because the process sounded horrible and I was just a kid. But now I accept my death—in whatever form it takes—as part of this journey. I think so many people are so afraid of death that they don't allow themselves to enjoy life, and I find this sad.

—**Shawn Decker,** hemophiliac and HIV/AIDS educator, *on coping with having HIV from a blood transfusion*

Fighting prostate cancer, having to accept the fact that you had cancer—my father died of prostate cancer—having to figure out how to deal with it, had a big impact on me. It probably helped a lot to understand some of what people were going through on September 11—having to face mortality, having to face death, having to face these perplexing questions of why someone is alive and why someone else is dead. . . . Those are the questions that perplex human beings. And when you have to face that in your life, you either grow or you recede. And I think that having prostate cancer helped me to grow, philosophically, religiously. . . .

—Rudolph Giuliani, politician and attorney, *on recovering from prostate cancer and the September 11, 2001, terrorist attacks*

The question is, Who are we sad for? In materialism you get an extra edge of sadness if you think that all that the person you loved had was their body, and their life becomes nothing after they die. But you can't be that sad, because they simply don't exist. They don't mind that they don't exist. They don't even remember that they ever did. Still, you feel kind of sad, because maybe someone died young, or maybe something was left undone. And personally you miss them, so you're sad for yourself. Why not? I must admit that when I finally came to grasp the issue of the boundlessness of life, that is, that death and birth don't bound life, I found it very helpful in regard to people dying.

—Robert Thurman, Buddhist scholar

. . . As you get older, loss is everywhere. We can't get away from it. And the more you acknowledge loss, the more you can really experience the bittersweet joy of how fleeting life is.
—*Diane Keaton,* actress and director

Remind yourself that as individuals and even as a species, life is limited and precious. Enjoy your life and strive to understand yourself and your purpose while you have the chance.

After sleeping through a hundred million centuries we have finally opened our eyes on a sumptuous planet, sparkling with color, bountiful with life. Within decades we must close our eyes again. Isn't it a noble, an enlightened way of spending our brief time in the sun, to work at understanding the universe and how we have come to wake up in it?
—*Richard Dawkins,* evolutionary biologist

SELECTED SOURCES

ACCEPTING

Winfrey: "Her Husband Tried to Kill Her Three Times." *The Oprah Winfrey Show,* October 21, 2005.

Shriver: "Q&A With Maria Shriver." CBS News. 25 December 2004. Online: http://www.cbsnews.com/stories/2004/03/23/48hours/main608242.shtml.

Siegel: "Accept, Retreat & Surrender: How to Heal Yourself." Shareguide. November 12, 2006. Online: http://www.shareguide.com/Siegel.html.

Crow: "Sheryl Crow Says Armstrong Didn't Abandon Her When She Was Ill." *Good Morning America,* July 6, 2006.

Allende: Baldock, Bob, & Dennis Bernstein. "Skirting the Brink: America's Leading Thinkers and Activists Confide Their Views of Our Predicament." *Mother Jones,* September/October 1994.

Simon: Kors, Michael. "Carly Simon: Romance, Pain, Anticipation—If It's a Human Impulse, Then Carly Simon Has Sung About It." *Interview,* July 2004.

L'Engle: L'Engle, Madeleine. Commencement address. Wellesley University, Wellesley, Massachusetts, July 15, 1999.

Flagg: Mills, Nancy. "Interview with Fannie Flagg: Q&A." Spirited Woman.com. April 23, 2007. Online: http://www.creativity-portal.com/bc/nancy.mills/ flagg.html.

Warren: "Encore Presentation: Interview with Pat Boone's Family." *Larry King Live*, January 4, 2003.

Brehony: Brehony, Kathleen. *After the Darkest Hour: How Suffering Begins the Journey to Wisdom*. New York: Henry Holt, 2001.

Farrow: Sischy, Ingrid. "Mia Farrow—actress— Interview." *Interview*, April 1994.

Getty: Baroni, Diane. "A Young Man with a Dark Past and Bright Future." November 21, 2006. Online: http://www.moviecrazed.com/outpast/ getty.html.

Amos: Gabriella. "Interview with Tori Amos." *NY Rock*, June 1998. Online: http://www.nyrock.com/ interviews/toriamos.htm. Accessed November 30, 2006.

Wells: "Rebecca Wells on Ya-Yas in Bloom." HarperCollins.com. November 21, 2006. Online: http://www.harpercollins.com/ (search: Wells).

BELIEVING

Knight: "Gladys Knight Talks About Her New Look and Play, 'Smokey Joe's Café.'" *Jet*, February 7, 2000.

Bronson: "We're All in Search of a Sense of Family." Interview by Wendy Schuman. Beliefnet.com. October 12, 2006. Online: http://www.beliefnet. com/story/180/story_18017_1.html.

Jennings: "Peter Jennings Discusses 'The Search for Jesus'." *Larry King Live*, June 15, 2000.

Taylor: Taylor, Susan. "Lessons in Living—excerpted from 'Lessons in Living'." *Essence*, December 1995.

Turlington: "The Model Yogini." Interview by Anne Simpkinson. Beliefnet.com. October 12, 2006. Online: http://www.beliefnet.com/story/86/story_8649.html.

Nye: Moyers, Bill. "Transcript: Naomi Shihab Nye." NOW. October 11, 2002. Online: http://www.pbs.org/now/transcript/transcript_nye.html. Accessed October 21, 2005.

Moyers: Moyers, William Cope. *Broken.* New York: Viking, 2006.

Adams: "The Wellness Show." Global Ideas Bank. July 8, 2006. Online: http://www.globalideasbank.org/site/bank/idea.php?ideaId=935.

Estefan: "Interview with Gloria Estefan." Interview by Marc Fest. Marcfest.com. September 8, 1988. Online: http://www.marcfest.com/festnet/htdocs/marc/estefan/. Accessed November 30, 2006.

McGinnis: Nozizwe, Lena. "The Power of Optimism—Interview with Psychotherapist Alan Loy McGinnis." *Vibrant Life,* May–June 1991.

Wiseman: Pink, Daniel. "How to Make Your Own Luck." *Fast Company,* June 2003.

CHANGING

Burroughs: Burroughs, Augusten. *Dry: A Memoir.* New York: St. Martin's Press, 2003.

Nemcova: "Encore Presentation: Interview with Petra Nemcova." *Larry King Live.* May 22, 2005.

Seymour: "Near Death Experiences." *Larry King Live,* May 23, 2005.

Kitano: "Takeshi Kitano." Asian Film Foundation.com. Online: http://www.asianfilm.org/modules.php?name=Encyclopedia&op=content&tid=70.

Somers: "Interview with Actress Suzanne Somers." *Larry King Live,* March 14, 2004.

Jobs: Jobs, Steve. Commencement address, Stanford University, Stanford, CA. June 14, 2005.

Pinkett-Smith: "Jada Pinkett-Smith." Interview by Tom Cruise. *Interview,* August 2004.

Vanzant: "Iyanla Vanzant Discusses Things She's Grateful for." Interview by Tavis Smiley. National Public Radio (NPR), November 28, 2002.

Clooney: "A Candid Conversation. . . ." Interview by Bernard Weinraub. *Playboy,* July 2000.

Johnson: "Cookie Johnson on: The Magic 'miracle': 'The Lord has healed Earvin.'" Interview by Laura B. Randolph. *Ebony,* April 1997.

Shue: "Elisabeth Shue—actress—Interview." Interview by Graham Fuller. *Interview,* March 1996.

Chopra: "Healing After the September 11 Attacks." *Larry King Live,* January 2, 2002.

Wilde: Wilde, Oscar. *De Profundis* (1853) New York: Penguin Classics. 1976.

Fry: Netdoctor.com. "Interviews with Stephen Fry, Winona Ryder and Stan Collymore on fame, fortune and depression." February 2000. Online: http://community.netdoktor.com.

Winterson: "Jeanette Winterson, England's Literary Outlaw Talks About the Erotics of Quantum Physics and The Horrors of the British Press." Interview by Laura Miller. *Salon Magazine.* April 1997. Online: http://www.salon.com/april97/winterson970428. html.

Brehony: Brehony, Kathleen. *After the Darkest Hour: How Suffering Begins the Journey to Wisdom.* New York: Henry Holt, 2001.

Scorsese: "The Inner Scorsese—director Martin Scorsese—Interview." Interview by Graham Fuller. *Interview,* January 1998.

Seymour: "Near Death Experiences." *Larry King Live,* May 23, 2005.

Robbins: "Healing After the September 11 Attacks." *Larry King Live,* January 2, 2002.

Brooks: "An interview with David Allen Brooks." Interview by E.C. McMullen Jr.. David Allen Brooks.com. Online: http://www.davidallenbrooks. com/interview.htm. Accessed April 22, 2007.

Messner: "Interview with Tammy Faye Messner." *Larry King Live,* July 31, 2005.

Hamilton: "Scott Hamilton Interview." Academy of Achievement, October 18, 2006. Online: http://www.achievement.org/autodoc/page/ hamoint-4#hamo-o1o.

Thomas: "Marlo Thomas Discusses Her New Book: The Right Words at the Right Time." *Tim Russert Show,* May 27, 2006.

Stone: "Been There, Done That." Interview by Asha Bandele. *Essence,* March 2003.

Connelly: "Jennifer Connelly: How Holding out for Something That Mattered Paid off." Interview by Ingrid Sischy. *Interview,* April 2002.

Drescher: "Interview with Fran Drescher." *Larry King Live,* May 6, 2002.

Jamison: "Manic Depression." Interview by Geraldine Doogue. "Life Matters" *Radio National.* January 22, 2001. Online: http://www.abc.net.au/ rn/talks/lm/stories/s155463.htm.

Cosby: "Oprah's Cut with Camille Cosby." Interview by Oprah Winfrey. *O, The Oprah Magazine,* May/June 2000.

Williams: "Sunday Morning Improv." *Psychology Today*, July/August 1995. Online: http://www.psychologytoday.com/articles/pto-19950701-000018.html. Accessed November 30, 2006.

Cronkite: Cronkite, Kathy. *On the Edge of Darkness: Conversations About Conquering Depression*. New York: Delta, 2005.

Goleman: Goleman, Daniel. "Friends for Life: An Emerging Biology of Emotional Healing." *Social Intelligence*, November 8, 2006.

Dole: "Bob Dole Speaks out for Early Prostate Cancer Detection." Interview by Cory SerVaas. *Saturday Evening Post*, July–August, 1992.

Fox: "A Conversation with Michael J. Fox." *Stanford Medicine Magazine*, Fall 2004. Online: http://mednews.stanford.edu/stanmed/2004fall/fox.html. Accessed October 17, 2006.

Pauley: "Jane Pauley." Interview by Chet Cooper and Dr. Gillian Friedman. Abilitymagazine.com. Online: http://www.abilitymagazine.com/jane_pauley.html. Accessed November 30, 2006.

Wallace: "60 Minutes of Truth." Academy of Achievement, October 22, 2006. Online: http://www.achievement.org/autodoc/page/wal2int-7.

Slater: "Christian Slater: He's Got a New Life. Take a New Look." Interview by Scott Lyle Cohen. *Interview*, November 2001.

John: "Elton John: 150% Involved." Interview by Ingrid Sischy. *Interview*, April 1995.

Ulene: "Cindy McCain and Physicians Discuss Preventative Medicine." *Larry King Live*, August 23, 2000.

Spinney: ". . . to Sesame Street and Its Fine-feathered and Furry Creatures, Who've Taught Kids Everywhere About Being Human." Interview by Jeffrey Slonim. *Interview*, November 1994.

Fox: "The Ties That Bind: An Interview with Michael J. Fox." *Ladies Home Journal*, September 2006.

Lauer: "Matt Lauer: Interview Highlights." *Larry King Live*, April 1, 2001.

Ensler: "Interview with Eve Ensler." Interview by Marianne Schnall. Feminist.com. October 3, 2006. Online: http://www.feminist.com/resources/ artspeech/interviews/eveensler.html. Accessed December 26, 2006.

Etheridge: "Oprah Interviews Melissa Etheridge." *The Oprah Winfrey Show*, June 13, 2006.

Barrymore: "The Drew That Grew—Interview with Actress Drew Barrymore." Interview by Ingrid Sischy. *Interview*, May 1995.

CREATING

Tan: "A Life Stranger than Fiction." Interview by Helena de Bertodano. *Telegraph*, November 11, 2003. Online: http://www.telegraph.co.uk? (Path: Arts, Tan).

Jewel: "Jewel: Q: What's She Got to Do with It?" Interview by Ingrid Sischy. *Interview*, July 1997.

Berry: Dimanno, Rosie. "A chillingly familiar scene." *Toronto Star*. April 13, 2007.

Manning: "Interview with Greg and Lauren Manning." *Larry King Live*, October 21, 2002.

Wallace: "The Salon Interview: David Foster Wallace." Interview by Laura Miller. *Salon Magazine*. March 8, 1996. Online: http://www.salon.com/09/ features/wallace1.html.

McGovern: "Honest George—Interview with George McGovern." Interview by Mark Marvel. *Interview*, May 1996.

Anderson: "Interview with Musician Laurie Anderson." Interview by Germano Celant. *Interview,* August 1998.

Carey: "Entertainment Clipreels." AP Archives. Online: http://www.aparchive.com/aparchive/pages/ent/cent_carey.html. Accessed November 30, 2006.

Thomas: "Rob Thomas: He's Been on Top of the Charts, Ruled Modern Rock Radio, and Wrestled with Critics Who Have Called Him a Master of the Middlebrow." Interview by Bernie Taupin. *Interview,* May 2005.

Schnabel: "Basquiat—African-American painter Jean-Michel Basquiat." Interview by Ingrid Sischy. *Interview,* July 1996.

Fellini: "Federico Fellini: Great Half-and-a-Half." Interview by Liselotte Millauer. *Interview,* January 1994.

Delaney: "Topher Delaney's Broad Vision of the Role Gardens Can Play." *Morning Edition* (NPR), October 10, 2001 (Transcript).

Kushner: Kushner, Harold. *Living a Life That Matters.* New York: Knopf, 2001.

FORGIVING

Perry: "Films of Family, Faith, and Forgiveness." Interview by Michael Kress. Beliefnet.com, July 2006. Online: http://www.beliefnet.com/story/185/story_18587_1.html.

Barasch: "Body Language: A Conversation with Marc Ian Barasch on Illness and Healing." Interview by Derrick Jensen. Derrickjensen.org. January 2000. Online: http://www.derrickjensen.org/barasch.html. Accessed October 20, 2006.

Bell: Bell, Michael Davitt. "Magic Time." *Atlantic,* December 1996.

Tutu: "Forgiving the Unforgivable." Interview by Frank Ferrari. *Commonweal,* September 12, 1997.

Kor: "Speech Given by the Founder and President of Children of Auschwitz—Nazi's Deadly Lab Experiments Survivors" (C.A.N.D.L.E.S). Eva Mozes Kor on the occasion of the opening of the symposium entitled "Biomedical Sciences and Human Experimentation at Kaiser Wilhelm Institutes—The Auschwitz Connection." June 7, 2001. CANDLES Holocaust Museum. Online: http://www.candlesholocaustmuseum.org/index. php?sid=44. Accessed September 12, 2006.

Olivier: "An Interview with Olivier's Son, Director Richard Olivier." Interview by Ann McFerran. *London Times,* April 11, 1999.

Beah: "Ishmael Beah Was Never Very Far Away." Interview by Dave Weich. Powells.com. February 2007. Online: http://www.powells.com/interviews/ ishmaelbeah.html.

Cohen: Cohen, Darlene. *Finding a Joyful Life in the Heart of Pain.* Boston: Shambhala, 2000.

Lennon: "John Lennon and Yoko Ono." Interview by Robin Blackburn and Tariq Ali. *Red Mole.* Online: http://www.geocities.com/CapitolHill/Senate/6173/ lennonrm.htm. Accessed January 21, 1971.

Moore: Moore, Dinty. "The Accidental Buddhist." Beliefnet.com. Online: http://www.beliefnet.com/ story/22/story_2266_1.html. Accessed July 12, 2006.

Rinpoche: Rinpoche, Chagdud. "Hitting Your Head with a Hammer." Beliefnet.com, July 12, 2006. Online: http://www.beliefnet.com/story/22/ story_2271_1.html.

Luskin: "The Necessity of Forgiveness: An Interview with Dr. Fred Luskin." PBS.org. Online: http://www. pbs.org/kqed/onenight/stories/forgive/index.html. Accessed June 6, 2006.

Khan: "In new book, 'Chaka! Through the Fire,' singer talks about her battle with drugs, her poor choices of men, being an absentee mother, and how she learned to forgive herself." Interview by Clarence Waldron. *Jet*, December 22, 2003.

Angelou: "Laugh and Dare to Love: An Interview with Maya Angelou." Interview by Linda Wolf. *In Context*, Winter 1995/96.

LAUGHING

Rivers: "Smiling Through Triumph and Tragedy; Celebrities Tell Their Stories of Losing Loved Ones and the Long Journey Back to Healing After Their Loss." *The Geraldo Rivera Show*, August 22, 1997.

Vieira: "Meredith Vieira Talks About Husband's MS, Cancer Battles." Interview by Alan B. Goldberg. ABCNEWS.com. Online: http://abclocal.go.com/wls/story?section=News&id=1153944. Accessed October 12, 2006.

Kellogg: "An Interview with Steven Kellogg." Online: http://www.powells.com/cgi-bin/biblio?inkey=17-0688140424-0. Accessed December 8, 2006.

Douglas: "Interview with Kirk Douglas." Interview by Chet Cooper. Abilitymagazine.com. Online: http://www.abilitymagazine.com/douglas_interview.html. Accessed December 6, 2006.

Dibert-Fitko: "On Humor and Healing." Interview by Tammie Fowles. Sageplace.com. Online: http://sageplace.com/on_humor_and_healing.htm. Accessed December 8, 2006.

Vogelstein: "Bert Vogelstein Interview." Academy of Achievement. Online: http://www.achievement.org/autodoc/page/vogoint-1. Accessed October 22, 2006.

Gore: "Take It From Me: Al Gore." Interview by Bill Stieg. Men's Health. http://www.menshealth.com. Accessed April 23, 2007.

Ostrower: "Humor as a Defense Mechanism in the Holocaust." Dissertation. Tel Aviv University. January 2000. Online: http://web.macam98.ac.il/~ochayo/absractn.html. Accessed September 2, 2006.

LIVING

Schlesinger: "Live for Something Outside of Yourself." Interview by Dena Ross. Beliefnet.com. Online: http://www.beliefnet.com/story/190/story_19065_1.html. Accessed August 19, 2006.

John: "Elton John: 150% Involved." Interview by Ingrid Sischy. *Interview,* April 1995.

Kidman: "Madame Moulin." Interview by Jess Cagle. *Time,* May 6, 2001.

Jong: Jong, Erica. *Fear of Fifty: A Midlife Memoir.* New York: HarperCollins, 2006.

Chopra: "Quantum Healing." Interview by Daniel Redwood, DC. Healthy.net, 1995. Online: http://www.healthy.net/asp/templates/interview.asp?PageType=Interview&Id=167:. Accessed August 8, 2006.

Lynch: "The Magic of Meditation." Interview by Karen Springen. *Newsweek,* July 26, 2005.

PERSISTING

Lucas: "Author Talk." *Book Reporter.com.* October 2004. http://www.bookreporter.com/authors/au-lucas-geralyn.asp

King: "Montel Williams Discusses His Fight with Multiple Sclerosis." *Larry King Live,* August 24, 1999.

Danson: "Interview with Ted Danson." Interview by Marianne Schnall. Feminist.com, 1996. Online: http://www.feminist.com/resources/artspeech/interviews/ted.html. Accessed October 16, 2006.

Grove: "Taking on Prostate Cancer." Interviewed by Bethany McLean. *Time*, May 13, 1996.

Lamott: "Word by Word with Anne Lamott." Interview by Dave Weich. Powells.com. September 2003. Online: http://www.powells.com/authors/lamott.html.

Fisher: Fisher, Helen. *Why We Love*. New York: Henry Holt, 2004.

Moyers: Moyers, William Cope. *Broken*. New York: Viking, 2006.

Albright: "Tensley Albright Interview." Academy of Achievement, July 21, 1991. Online: http://www.achievement.org/autodoc/page/alboint-1. Accessed October 5, 2006.

TRANSCENDING

Nolte: "Has Award-Winning Actor Nick Nolte Found the Fountain of Youth?" *Larry King Live*, February 16, 2000.

Cope: "Coping, Not Coping and Mr. Cope." Interview by Ray Rogers. *Interview*, January 1996.

Stone: Williams, Kevin. "Near-Death Experiences of the Rich and Famous." Mind Power News. Online: http://www.mindpowernews.com/RichAndFamous.htm. Accessed October 31, 2006.

Cohen: "Leonard Cohen." Interview by Anjelica Huston. *Interview*, November 1995.

Nolte: "Nick Nolte, Acting the Wiser." Interview by Valerie Reiss. Beliefnet.com. Online: http://www.beliefnet.com/story/192/story_19246_1.html. Accessed August 9, 2006.

Chopra: "We Are the Thinker Behind the Thought." Interview with Dr. Deepak Chopra by Monte Leach. Accessnewage.com. Online: http://accessnewage.com/articles/mystic/Chopra.htm. Accessed September 10, 2006.

Dillard: Dillard, Annie. *The Pilgrim at Tinker Creek*. New York: Harper. 1998.

Sendak: "An Interview with Maurice Sendak." Interview by Roger Sutton. *The Horn Book Magazine,* November/December 2003.

Decker: Decker, Shawn. *My Pet Virus*. New York: Tarcher, 2006.

Giuliani: "Rudolph Giuliani." Academy of Achievement, May 3, 2002. Online: http://www.achievement.org/autodoc/page/giuoint-1.

Thurman: "Lust for Life: Bob Thurman." Interview by Dimitri Ehrlich. *Interview,* February 1996.

PERMISSIONS

Special thanks to the following for their permission to republish quotes in this book:

Chopra (pp. 213–14): "We Are the Thinker Behind the Thought." Interview with Dr. Deepak Chopra by Monte Leach. Monte Leach is a freelance radio journalist, based in San Francisco and is the U.S. editor of Share International. © Share International

Barasch (p. 129): "Body Language: A Conversation with Marc Ian Barasch on Illness and Healing." Interview by Derrick Jensen. Derrickjensen. org. January 2000. http://www.derrickjensen.org/barasch.html.

Dibert-Fitko (pp. 154–55): "On Humor and Healing." Interview by Tammie Fowles. Sageplace.com. December 8, 2006. http://sageplace.com/on_humor_and_healing.htm.

Kor (pp. 134–35): CandesHolocaustMuseum.com.

ACKNOWLEDGMENTS

Many thanks to Helena Santini, my editor, for acquiring *Healing* and for nursing it through its many incarnations. Thanks also to Sheryl Stebbins, Bistra Bogdanova, and Tigist Getachew at Random House. I would also like to thank several of the contributors for source material: Eva Kor, Tammie Fowles, Derrick Jensen, and Share International.